EXPLORING STRATFORD-UPON-AVON
Historical Strolls around the town

John Abbott

Copyright © John Abbott, 1997

All Rights Reserved. No part of this publication may be reproduced, stored in a retrieval system, or transmitted in any form or by any means – electronic, mechanical, photocopying, recording, or otherwise – without prior written permission from the publisher.

Published by Sigma Leisure – an imprint of
Sigma Press, 1 South Oak Lane, Wilmslow, Cheshire SK9 6AR, England.

British Library Cataloguing in Publication Data
A CIP record for this book is available from the British Library.

ISBN: 1-85058-463-X

Typesetting and Design by: Sigma Press, Wilmslow, Cheshire.

Cover photograph: Anne Hathaway's Cottage (by permission, The Shakespeare Birthplace Trust)

Maps by: the author

Photographs by: David Medcroft

Printed by: MFP Design & Print

Disclaimer: the information in this book is given in good faith and is believed to be correct at the time of publication. No responsibility is accepted by either the author or publisher for errors or omissions, or for any loss or injury howsoever caused. Only you can judge your own fitness, competence and experience.

Acknowledgments: I would like to thank the Stewarts for their support. I am grateful to Mairi Macdonald M.A., D.A.A., of Stratford's Records Office, who took the time and trouble to check the manuscript.

A Dedication: for Phyllis

Contents

Introduction		1
The Bard		9
Walk 1:	Central Stratford (1)	14
Walk 2:	Central Stratford (2)	21
Walk 3:	Central Stratford (3)	29
Walk 4:	Central Stratford (4)	38
Walk 5:	Central Stratford (5)	42
Walk 6:	Shottery – Anne Hathaway's Cottage	49
Walk 7:	Environs (1)	55
Walk 8:	Environs (2)	59
Walk 9:	Luddington	63
Walk 10:	Welford-on-Avon and Weston-on-Avon	68
Walk 11:	Clifford Chambers	74
Walk 12:	Preston-on-Stour	82
Walk 13:	Snitterfield	87
Walk 14:	Wilmcote – Mary Arden's House	96
Walk 15:	Aston Cantlow	103
Walk 16:	Charlecote	109

Introduction

This book describes sixteen walks in Stratford and the surrounding countryside. Cautiously quilled on the straight and narrow, a three-pronged Elizabethan arrow, it is aimed at the hearts, minds and legs of visitors and walkers: people intent upon sampling a huge slice of English Heritage, who also want to exercise those parts of the body that William Shakespeare may not reach.

There are five Central walks: they weave in and around, wherever possible making use of zebras and other pedestrian crossings. Stratford can be very busy, particularly in the summer months, and it makes sense to keep a wary eye open for traffic. The prologues summarise many of the places passed *en route*. A sketch map is provided with every walk, but for the first five (at least), you may find a town map useful. The Tourist Information Centre in Bridgefoot stocks a free map and Travel Guide. Do not feel constrained by my efforts: it is easy to wander off course, perhaps even deliberately, joining another of the walks within the town; it is quite difficult to get lost, though.

Anne Hathaway's Cottage at Shottery is the focus of Walk 6: an easy, linear fifteen minutes from Evesham Place (extending Walk 5), with the Guide Friday bus, nearby, should you feel the need.

The two Environs walks are so called because they do not concentrate on anything in particular; except, perhaps, exercise and watery views. One is measured in minutes, the other in miles. Distance, terrain and so forth are to be found in the prologues.

Lastly, there are eight walks in the surrounding countryside. One passes alongside the Stratford-upon-Avon Canal to Mary Arden's House at Wilmcote; others perambulate through attractive villages, often lined with timber-framed, thatched houses in their 'natural', lived-in state. The occasional church is passed and a brief description is given. The Guide Friday bus stops at Wilmcote. A bus is also possible with the other walks but always refer to the Travel Guide, bearing in mind distance and timing. You may decide to invest in O.S. Landranger 151 or O.S. Pathfinders 997 and 998; they give a better overall picture.

The Shakespeare Birthplace Trust administers the five Shakespearean properties: the Henley Street Birthplace, New Place/Nash's House in Chapel Street, Hall's Croft along Old Town, Anne Hathaway's Cottage at Shottery and Mary Arden's House in Wilmcote. Prices of entry vary, but if you intend (while walking) to visit all five, an economy move is to buy an inclusive ticket. The Trust is based within the Shakespeare Centre in Henley Street and may be contacted on 01789 204016.

I have not included everything of interest in Stratford (this would require a book of doormat proportions). The detail is far from comprehensive, being for walkers and visitors, not academics, though I have always tried to resolve 'contradictions' found when researching and had the manuscript checked.

From Walk 8 onwards, dress sensibly. Pack a waterproof – weather forecasts have been known to be wrong. Boots that have been worn a few times, proven 'blister free', are recommended. Woollen socks are a good idea, as well. There are hardly any gradients but plenty of mud in the winter months, and miles of stiles. The prologues give the necessary detail.

Respect the countryside: guard against risk of fire; stay on the paths; keep dogs under control; do not disturb livestock; close gates (unless obviously meant to be open); avoid damage to crops, fences, hedges, trees; leave no litter; and take care of yourself, especially along roads, using the pavement or grass verge.

I apologise in advance should you find that a walk does not correspond with my description. While every care has been taken in the compilation of this book, the author cannot accept responsibility for any errors. With time, everything changes (even the changes) – freshly ploughed fields, new stiles, gates, a diversion, church detail – anything can happen, and sometimes does.

Stating the obvious: getting out and about, not just being carried hither and yon, will do you good. The walking is as important as the looking, adding another dimension to Stratford. Meticulously exercise all parts – cast around and plot – and make your visit to the town a truly memorable experience.

General Information

Access: Road map in hand, it is not too difficult to work out a route, and once on the road, you will find that Stratford is well-signed. But do not rely on the map completely, for cartographers wage a losing battle against change: road works are everywhere these days. Three of many possibilities via the M5 are:

Take the M42 at junction 4A. Approaching the M40, signed Warwick, London and Stratford, keep to the two right-hand lanes, moving ahead along the M40 at junction 3A. Later, leave the M40 at junction 16, opting for the A3400, signed Henley. An attractive ride that goes through Henley-in-Arden and

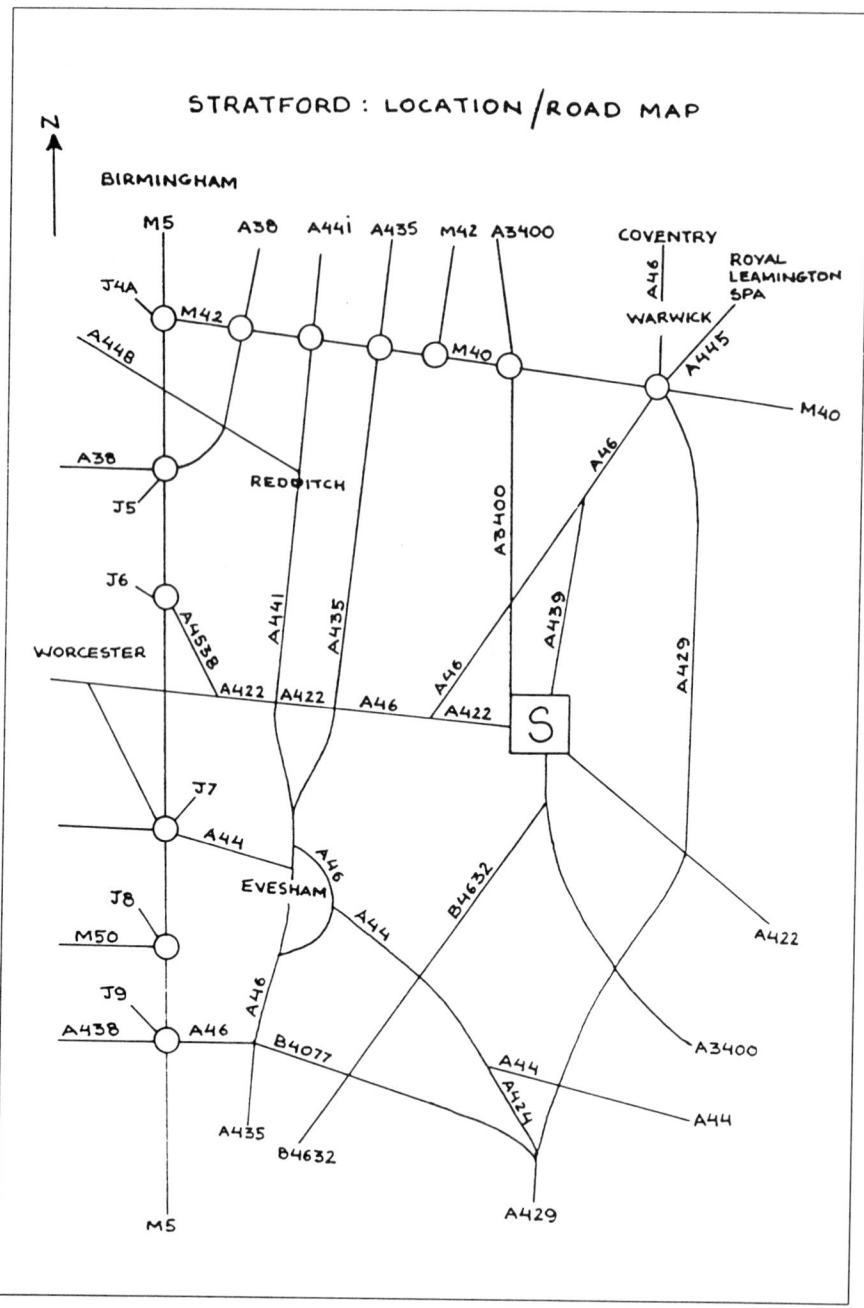

Introduction

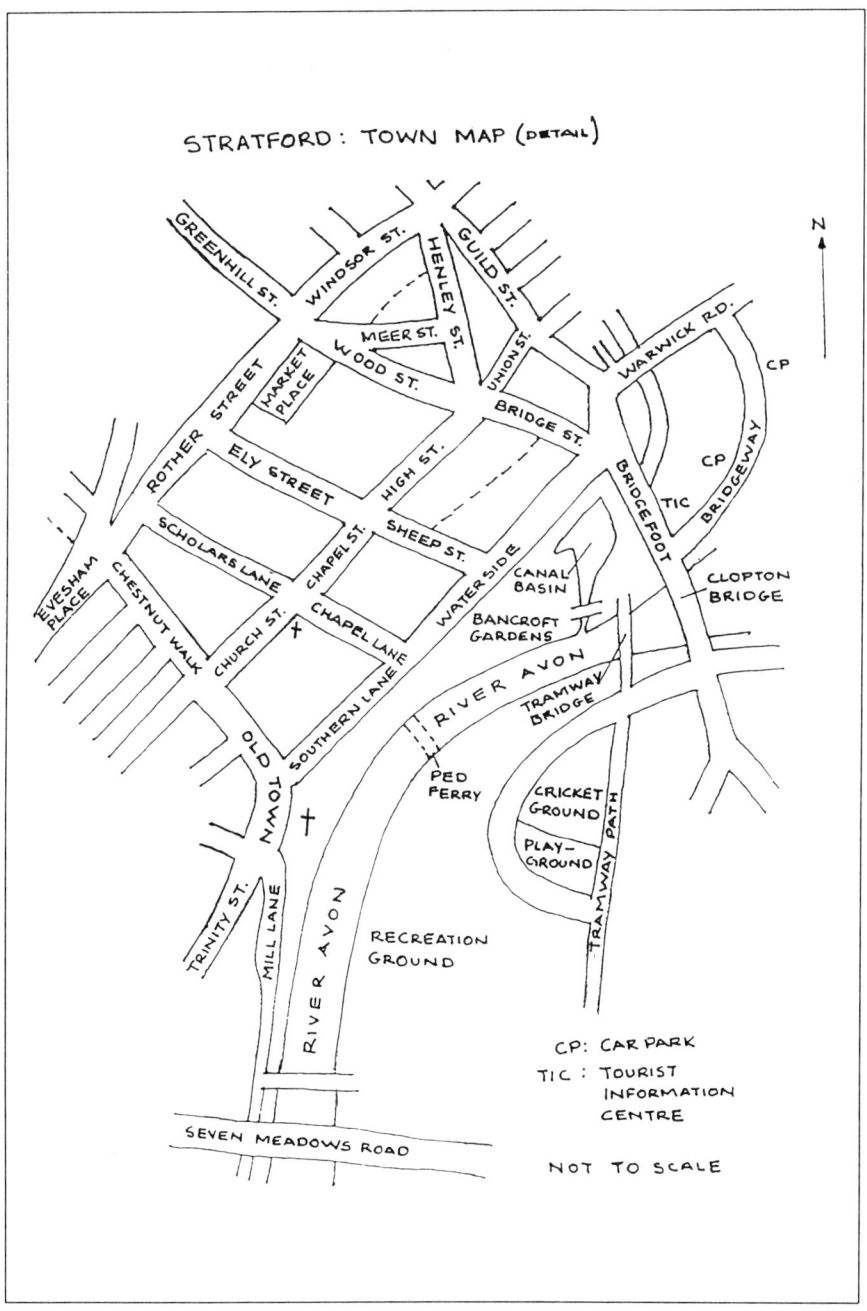

under Wootton Wawen's aqueduct. Follow the Stratford, and then the Town Centre signs, still on the A3400, signed Shipston, now.

Leaving junction 7, select (initially) the A44, signed Worcester – ordeal by roundabout – following the Stratford signs from then on. One such puts you onto the A46; a final stretch of A422 brings you to Stratford. Stay with the Town Centre signs – Alcester Road, passing the railway station – Greenhill Street – Wood Street – Bridge Street, the end of which becomes one-way. Further, move across to the two right-hand lanes, the A3400, signed Shipston.

At the junction 9 exit, choose the A46, signed and eventually bypassing Evesham. Continue along the A46 – dual carriageways, roundabouts and an encouraging: 'Welcome to Warwickshire Shakespeare's County' sign, complete with Bear and Ragged Staff – as before, changing to the A422 and entering Stratford, a Beautiful Britain in Bloom winner.

Mobile nourishment: Why not try one of the roadside eating establishments along the way? Treat yourself to a pre-walk pot of tea or coffee, and there may be a newspaper to read. Fruit farms line the roads, offering 'pickables' in season: freshly-plucked raspberries to juicily stimulate the taste buds. Prudence is a flask and sandwich in a lay-by.

Parking: It is not easy to find a free place, so it is more convenient to use a Pay and Display (have a few pound coins handy). There are several P & Ds in the town; the two I mention fit in reasonably well with many of the walks. Continuing Access: in Stratford, following the A3400, signed Shipston, beyond where the lanes curve right, you come to open-air Riverside on your left; then only a few metres further on your right, multistorey Bridgefoot. Bridgefoot is better in the sense that it is slightly nearer the Tourist Information Centre (TIC) and has Public Toilets.

Introduction

Public Transport: Stratford is quite well-off as regards bus and train services. Notwithstanding the Beeching cuts of the sixties, the town still has a railway station. It is situated in Station Road, close to where Alcester Road becomes Greenhill Street. The other end of Greenhill Street is touched upon in Walk 5. Train timetables are available from the TIC. Train enquiries are on 0345-484950.

The TIC stocks a free Travel Guide which you may find of use when walking the walks as well as getting to Stratford in the first place. In it you will read about:

National Express coaches 'linking hundreds of places throughout the UK', including a daily service between Stratford and London. All enquiries to 0990-808080.

Stratford Blue for 'regular services in and around Stratford-upon-Avon'. Timetables and places served are given. Invaluable during a walk in the country when the heavens open, or when half a walk is enough. Try the National Express number (see above) or 01788 535555.

The Guide Friday open-topped double-deckers will take you to many of the places of interest in and around Stratford, and provide a commentary, as well. They start outside the TIC (leaflet available), and there are stops dotted throughout the town. Their Tourism Centre is in the Civic Hall, 14 Rother Street, which is passed in Walk 5. They may be contacted on 01789 294466.

Refreshments: Everywhere – especially during the Central Walks and often mentioned in the prologues when out in the country. For aficionados of traditional fish and chips, the best for me were from the Greenhill Fish Bar in Greenhill Street (where the teddy bears go for their picnics).

Public Toilets: Almost everywhere and often mentioned in passing.

TIC: The Tourist Information Centre in Bridgefoot is the start of many of the walks and a good starting place for your visit. There have loads of leaflets and, as shown by the notices above the counter: 'Bus and Coach, General Enquiries, Accommodation, Book a Bed Ahead' and 'Foreign Exchange Services'. There is a small shop on one side. On request, they will send you free copies of an Accommodation Guide and a booklet on the town; also the Travel Guide if you ask for it. The town booklet contains a map showing the location of car parks and toilets. The multi-language General Information and Map leaflet is even better in this respect. A number to ring is 01789 293127.

Where to stay: Try the TIC. They have a 'Stop Over' leaflet giving details of available packages – see the sights, watch a play, a meal after and stay the night, for example. Naturally, you will want to fit in a few walks, so book an extra night or two. The quieter times of the year are to be preferred. This is when the 'vacancies' signs go up outside many of the numerous guest houses in the town, and when a DIY stay is easily arranged. Between spring and autumn, however, it is best to book a bed ahead.

The Bard

Introduction

Yet another article about William Shakespeare! Repeating the repeats: it has been done before, many times, and will no doubt be done again, many times; penned by scholars in radiant prose, far superior to this minor effort. A prelude to a view of the Bard, Stratford and its surrounds through the medium of sixteen walks helps to set this book in context. The majority of the walks have some sort of Shakespearean connection; it would be impossible for them not to have in Stratford. These I have briefly described in passing; for example, chronologically: Walk 5 takes in the Birthplace; Walk 3, the Grammar School; Walk 6 browses Anne Hathaway's Cottage at Shottery; then back to Walk 3 which also visits the Site of New Place, and finally Walk 2's Holy Trinity Church.

Important chapters in people's lives start at birth, proceed through work to retirement, and conclude with death. In this instance, Shakespeare's writing work took place in Elizabethan London, not Stratford. A trek too far, but certainly deserving of a mention, albeit in a book of Stratford walks.

Shakespeare in London

It is not really known exactly when Shakespeare left Stratford for London, though it was some time after 1585 following the birth of Hamnet and Judith. However, by 1592, he was working in the city's theatres as an actor and playwright.

In those days, actors belonged to a company of players: a form of co-operative in which they invested time and money (and not inconsiderable talent) in collectively owned properties, costumes, plays (bought from a playwright) and so forth. In effect, each participated in the costs and money made in proportion to share capital owned. These 'sharers' as they were known also engaged other actors when necessary.

Some theatres were rented; others owned. The Theatre (a theatre) was erected by James Burbage in April of 1576 on a twenty-one-year leased site north of Bishopsgate. With the lease due to expire in April, 1597, the wooden building was dismantled in some haste in December, 1598, and in January of 1599, work started (using the same timber) on The Globe. This theatre opened on the south bank of the Thames, south of Maid Lane, later in the same year. William Shakespeare was a 'sharer' in what was then called the Lord Chamberlain's Men, and which became the King's Men when James I, the son of Mary, Queen of Scots, succeeded Elizabeth I in 1603 and gave them his support. The Bard stayed with the company until his final return to Stratford's New Place in 1610.

Pity the poor actors: plagued by the plague, when theatres frequently had to be closed and the company was compelled to travel the country to earn a crust; and persecuted by the Puritans, who considered the theatre immoral, particularly Sunday performances (how times have changed). They managed to shut down the theatres in 1642; and they did not open again until 1660 (the Restoration).

The Plays

I do not have the expertise to give an analysis of the works of William Shakespeare; this would hardly be relevant here, anyway, even to rambling thespians. All I shall do is summarise snippets gathered from various sources. If you want to go into the subject in more depth, the Shakespeare Centre and Records Office are freely and helpfully available.

Surely the finest playwright ever? Prolific writer of comedies, histories and tragedies, charged with telling perception and power that rarely fail to stir the emotions – eternally, universally popular. How many other dramatists' works are open to virtually infinite interpretation in any language? What actor worth his salt has not tackled the part of Hamlet? Suffice to say that William wrote a good play, a passable poem and an acceptable sonnet.

There are no original manuscripts of Shakespeare's works in existence today, only one or two doubtful possibilities in the Apocrypha which consists of plays attributed to him but not included in the First Folio (see below). Additionally, the Apocrypha contains works to which he may have contributed, for example, Sir Thomas More. But, generally, it is believed that nothing authentic exists, and it follows that the definite chronological order of his works is also unknown, although scholars have deduced one from external and internal evidence.

The First Folio, published in 1623, represented the authorised complete Canon of thirty-six of William Shakespeare's 'Comedies, Histories and Tragedies'. They were assembled by his friends and fellow-actors, John Heminge and Henry Condell. The three sections add up to more than nine hundred pages. Approximately one thousand copies were printed and around 200 remain. Three further folios were published in later years, each attempting improvements (the English language evolved considerably during the Elizabethan age) and each, inevitably, generating more mistakes.

For completeness, listed below are the thirty-six plays in the First Folio. Troilus and Cressida was a late addition to the Tragedy section, and did not appear in the Folio's Catalogue.

The Comedies
The Tempest.
The Two Gentlemen of Verona.
The Merry Wives of Windsor.
Measure for Measure.
The Comedy of Errors.
Much Ado About Nothing.
Love's Labour's Lost.
A Midsummer Night's Dream.
The Merchant of Venice.
As You Like It.
The Taming of the Shrew.
All's Well That Ends Well.
Twelfth Night.
The Winter's Tale.

The Histories
King John.
Richard II.
Henry IV, Part I.
Henry IV, Part II.
Henry V.
Henry VI, Part I.
Henry VI, Part II.
Henry VI, Part III.
Richard III.
Henry VIII.

The Tragedies
Coriolanus.
Titus Andronicus.
Romeo and Juliet.
Timon of Athens.
Julius Caesar.
Macbeth.
Hamlet.

King Lear.
Othello.
Antony and Cleopatra.
Cymbeline.
Troilus and Cressida.

As a visitor to Stratford, you may well know them, and, of course, you will doubtless be looking forward to an evening in one of the town's theatres. But, standing in the foyer, and feeling the lack, you may find notes regarding character and plot useful.

In Conclusion

The busy Bard; familiar with parchment, paper, 'wing of goose' and ink, scratching his way into history. Genius and quality apart, an incredible output when compared to the relatively easy word processing of today. Incredible, too, that none of his plays, quilled in his own hand, survives.

Walk 1: Central Stratford (1)

Route: TIC – two pedestrian crossings – Canal Basin – Tramway Bridge – alongside the Avon – Witter Lock – Tramway Path – Tramway Bridge – TIC.

Start: The TIC in Bridgefoot.

What you will see: The Gower Memorial; The Tramway Bridge; Cox's Island; Clopton Bridge; The Pedestrian Ferry; The Colin P. Witter Lock; Stratford Butterfly Farm.

The Walk

From the TIC, walk approximately west, past the Pen and Parchment and entrance to Bancroft Place, keeping to the right-hand side, as far as the road bridge over the canal. Go left over the first pedestrian crossing (always keeping a wary eye open for traffic) to the traffic island. A signpost defines the known Shakespearean Universe. Here, take the second pedestrian crossing on your left, direction south, again going left (the right-hand pavement). After a few metres, turn right, down steps, towards the Canal Basin (described in Walk 2). Bearing left, brings you to:

The Gower Memorial

'This monument was unveiled on 10th October, 1888 ...' and is by Lord Ronald Gower. The Bard in bronze, above, plotting his next masterpiece, and four corner statues, below:

Prince Hal: 'Consideration like an angel came and whipt the offending Adam out of him.'

Prince Hal (Gower Memorial)

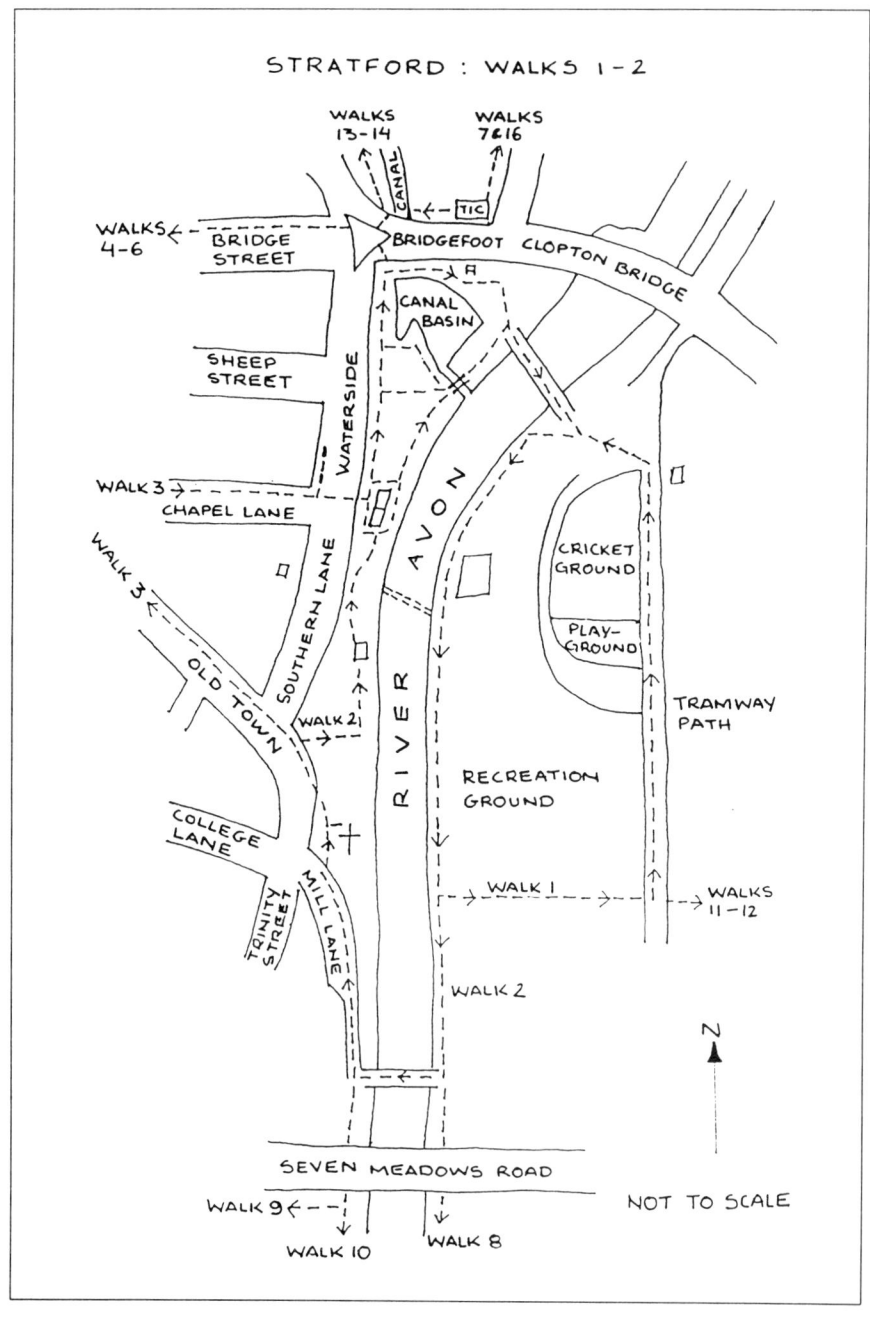

Falstaff: 'I am not only witty myself, but the cause that wit is in other men.'

Lady Macbeth: 'Life's but a walking shadow, a poor player that struts and frets his hour upon the stage and then is heard no more.'

Hamlet (said by Hamlet's friend Horatio on Hamlet's death): 'Good night, sweet prince, and flights of angels sing thee to thy rest!'

As an aside: Lady Macbeth and Hamlet have the best view, though Hamlet contemplates, more interested in Yorick's skull.

Try and resist the temptation to wander over to the nearby footbridge and Avon/Canal Lock (looked at in Walk 2), continuing to the end of the Canal Basin – executing a swift left, east, then right, south – to the start of:

The Tramway Bridge

This brick bridge across the River Avon, has nine arches and was built in 1823. It formed part of the tramway between Stratford and Moreton-in-Marsh. The tramway was opened in 1826; subsequently, horse-drawn wagons carried goods to and fro (off/onloaded at the Canal Basin). A bit far to walk, but in Shipston-on-Stour, which lies along the former route, one may see buildings and sidings, remnants of a terminus opened in 1836.

Proceed along the Tramway Bridge. To your left, Cox's Island, a nature reserve, beyond which you can see:

Clopton Bridge

There are fourteen arches to count on this bridge, which was built by Hugh Clopton towards the end of the fifteenth century.

The tower to the north-west once served as a toll-house and dates from 1814. The Clopton Chapel is viewed in Holy Trinity Church (Walk 2). You will get a closer look at the toll-house when you get around to (easy) Walk 7.

At the far side of the Tramway Bridge, go immediately right, and along, eventually bearing left by the River Avon. Swans cruise and preen as you walk south-west enjoying the display. On the far bank is the Theatre Complex, with the 'RSC' flag flying. You soon pass the bowling green, smooth as a snooker table, and the opportunity (not in the winter months), for a few pence, to cross the water (joining Walk 2) at the Pedestrian Ferry. You may also be able to make out on the far side of the river, The Other Place, one of three theatres in Stratford, and further along, the east end of Holy Trinity Church with its battlements, pinnacles, tower and recessed spire. A few metres more offers views of the Colin P. Witter Lock which was completed in 1974.

Swans being fed

Clopton Bridge

Before the footbridge, near the lock, bear left along the path by the edge of the Recreation Ground to weave roughly east, to the arch of the bridge that carries the Tramway Path. Here, take the path to your left, up to the TP, and then proceed left, north, back into the town. The path is straight and level, as a tramway should be; no horse-drawn wagons now, just Shanks's pony. The steps on your right lead to the Old Tramway Inn, eventually coming to:

Stratford Butterfly Farm

Well worth a visit: another 'live' theatre, in a way – 'fluttermime' – home of the daylight *Lepidoptera*. One such, a giant, hovers above the entrance. Inside, it is what one may call hot, ideal for the butterflies, insects, spiders and so forth. A tasty treat for many birds, but not the zebra finches, for example, that provide the background choral music. According to a leaflet, it is Europe's largest butterfly farm, and open every day except Christmas Day.

Note the building to the west which has signs to Public Toilets. Finally, cross the road and Tramway Bridge, back to the TIC.

Walk 2: Central Stratford (2)

Route: As Walk 1 to the Witter Lock – footbridge over the Avon – Mill Lane – Holy Trinity churchyard – Royal Shakespeare Theatre Gardens – Bancroft Gardens – Canal Basin – TIC.

Start: The TIC in Bridgefoot.

What you will see: Holy Trinity Church; The Brass Rubbing Centre; The Other Place; The Dirty Duck/Black Swan; The Swan Theatre; The Royal Shakespeare Theatre; The Avon/Canal Lock; Bancroft Gardens; The Canal Basin.

The Walk

NOTE: for this walk, please refer to the map for Walk 1.

This route leaves the first walk near the Colin P. Witter Lock, going ahead, across the footbridge over the stream, with the lock to your right. Further on, you come to the first of two weirs – after heavy November rains looking and sounding quite impressive. Pass the second weir, reaching the footbridge over the River Avon.

On this side, etched in wood, is the Stratford to Marlcliff footpath. Cross the footbridge, bearing right along the tarmac path and right-hand brick pavement of Mill Lane. Continue past Soli House, a Catholic Youth Retreat and, where Mill Lane curves left, by Avonfield, go ahead, into the churchyard. Pause, and perhaps wonder about the twisted tree trunk, looking like a giant pine bonsai, then go around to the north porch of:

Holy Trinity Church

A leaflet (the price of entry into the chancel) gives the necessary detail, including times of opening and services. However, for walkers, a browsing is irresistible.

Standing before the north porch and looking east, up at the tower, are battlements, with a pinnacle at each corner, topped by a recessed spire. Inside the porch, a notice welcomes you to: '... this house of God'. The leaflet describes the thirteenth century sanctuary ring on the inner door. Another notice warns about the (very) low door. Mind your head.

Enter and, on the right, a bookstall offers souvenirs and a guide book. Above the bookstall, on the north wall, you can see the Royal Arms of the Stuarts.

At the west end, look for: the font (its predecessor is in the chancel); a painting of the church as it was in the nineteenth century; also notes and photographs in a glass cabinet: 'In everloving memory of Vivienne (Bunny) Hudson-Evans 1910-1978', telling you about the building/rebuilding of the church, in particular, the chancel.

Arcades run north and south of the nave, each with six bays and six-sided piers. A clerestory rises above. Much attractive stained glass, around 100 years old, is everywhere, though there is some medieval glass in the Clopton Chapel. The windows are described in the leaflet.

Looking along the nave, you can see how the chancel is slightly 'offset' (read about this in the leaflet). The nave and aisles date from around 1300. There used to be balconies on the north and south sides.

Moving to the south aisle and walking east, you come to the Chapel of Thomas à Becket which has a triple sedilia set in the south wall. The nearby pulpit of green marble, with carvings on five of its sides, was donated by Sir Theodore Martin in memory of his wife, the actress, Helen Faucit.

Recross the nave to the Clopton Chapel (no entry). On the right, the south side of the chapel, stands the tomb chest of Hugh Clopton (1496). He built New Place and rebuilt Clopton Bridge, also the nave of the Guild Chapel (see Walk 3). Although a tomb is here, Hugh Clopton was buried in St Margaret's, Lothbury, London. He was Mayor of London in 1491-92. The other tomb chests are: the north side, with effigies, William Clopton (1592), his wife Anne, and children; the east side, The Earl of Totnes (1629) and his wife Joyce Clopton.

You come back to where you purchased the leaflet, as previously mentioned.

Adjacent to the Clopton Chapel is a silver Processional Cross: '... given to the church ... by the Shakespeare Memorial Theatre Company in memory of their fellow actor Frank Rodney ...'

Under the tower, looking up at the brass chandelier, one can just make out the year: 1720, I think. To left and right, the transepts, comprising the oldest part of the church, date from 1210. St Peter's Chapel on the south side is: 'set aside for prayer'.

And so to the chancel which, remembering the glass cabinet against the west wall, was rebuilt towards the end of the fifteenth century during Dean Thomas Balsal's time as Rector (1485-1491).

On either side are the old choir stalls, circa 1500. Note particularly the carved wood of the misericords. Wandering around this area, you can pick out several interesting ones. On the south side: a husband birching his wife; on the north side: a naked woman on a stag, a camel; there are many more.

Continuing along the north side, examine the copies of baptismal and burial records of William Shakespeare. Nearby, stands the fifteenth century font (on a new pedestal) in which, by all accounts, Vicar John Bretchgirdle christened the Bard on 26th April, 1564.

Then follows a 'roped-off' section with a visual feast of monuments, gravestones and stained glass. On the north wall, the Bard in alabaster, quill in hand, erected between 1616 and 1623 and restored several times in succeeding centuries. Beyond, is the tomb chest of Dean Thomas Balsal (1491).

Notices describe the five gravestones set in the floor, from left to right: Anne Hathaway (1556-1623), William Shakespeare (1564-1616) with the famous curse, Thomas Nash (1593-1647), John Hall (1575-1635), Susanna Hall (1583-1649). The curse is as follows:

'Good frend for Jesus sake forbeare,
to digg the dust enclosed heare;
Bleste be ye man yt [that] spares thes stones,
and curst be he yt [that] moves my bones.'

The gravestone is anonymous. William Shakespeare died on 23rd April, 1616. His line ended with Elizabeth Hall.

The mensa of the High Altar is of Purbeck marble. On the south side are a piscina and a richly carved triple sedilia, both with ogee arches. Returning along this side to inspect a chained bible. The King James Bible of 1611 was renowned for its elegance and lucidity.

One feature, which you may find interesting: back in the nave, on the north wall, are three hatchments (a hatchment displays a deceased's complete coat of arms) to members of the Clopton family; originally, four used to hang in the Clopton Chapel. And that, briefly, is that – back to the bookstall, perhaps, and away.

Leaving the church, continue north along the path, between an avenue of pollarded lime-trees, attractively tinted in the autumn. You can see where the next generation of saplings have been planted in between. Finally, reading the lettering cut in the stone beneath your feet (near the gate): 'HEN-RICUS/HARDING/QUONDAM/VICARUS'. Henry Harding was a Vicar of Holy Trinity Church.

Proceed along the pavement, only a few metres, to where you go right, into the gardens: 'Property of the Royal Shakespeare Theatre'. Temporary toilets are to be found to your left in the busier months as you go ahead, east, towards the river bank. Following the path around to the left brings you to:

The Brass Rubbing Centre

A free leaflet, available from the TIC, tells you about brasses. And it is here that you may 'produce a beautiful brass rubbing'. This will look really good, hanging (framed) on a wall of your lounge. Admission is free. A reasonable charge is made for the paper and coloured waxes, and instruction is provided. If you do not want to spend the 'less than an hour' that it takes, ready-made rubbings may be purchased. According to the leaflet, the centre is open all week from Easter to October (though it has been closed in October).

Through the gate at the far end is journey's end for the Pedestrian Ferry. Opposite and to the left, slightly, is The Other Place, the third Shakespearean theatre, away from the main Theatre Complex, where contemporary works are often enacted.

Continuing along this right-hand side, a path by a stone wall, as you return to the river. On the far side of the road stands the dual Dirty Duck/Black Swan. Looking at the inn sign: I wonder why the black swan looks as sober as a judge while the 'pinted' duck definitely does not; maybe Charles Edward Flower has the answer (see later).

Approaching the Theatre Complex, go left to the road. The Arden Hotel is opposite, by the entrance to Chapel Lane, at the end of which, the tower of the Guild Chapel (to be visited in Walk 3) is visible.

The Swan and Royal Shakespeare Theatres

The Royal Shakespeare Theatre dates from 1932, but the first (albeit temporary) theatre goes way back to 1769, being built for David Garrick's festival of that year. All credit to the brewer, Charles Edward Flower, who in the 1870s financed the building of the Shakespeare Memorial Theatre. In 1926, this fell victim to fire, and within six years the Royal Shakespeare Theatre, that you see today, was constructed. The adjacent Swan Theatre was converted from the shell of the old theatre in 1986.

Go up the steps and into the Swan Theatre. On your left is a gift shop which leads into a Review Room; one could spend some time here, reading the press cuttings. Leaving, go right, on around to the Royal Shakespeare Theatre for another wander within. All's Well That Ends Well: this is where you can buy a theatre ticket to round off the day. The Swan's ticket office usually does not open until the evening. The theatre's Box Tree Restaurant offers nourishment and fine views; toilets, too.

Leaving the theatre, continue by the river – chubby ducks, migrating geese and swans being fed – to the Avon/Canal Lock (number 56), the only wide beam lock of the canal, where the canal 'locks out' to the Avon. Watching a narrow boat pass through is a slow yet interesting routine – the first time, anyway. Standing on the footbridge: '... constructed by men

The Royal Shakespeare Theatre

from HM Prison Wormwood Scrubs and HM Prison Birmingham, 1961-1964 ... canal reopened by Queen Elizabeth The Queen Mother 11th July, 1964.'

Crossing, one may return via the Gower Memorial to the TIC. Alternatively, go north-west alongside the Canal Basin with its narrow boats, a narrow restaurant and the surrounding Bancroft Gardens.

Bancroft Gardens and the Canal Basin

Bancroft Gardens dates from the Middle Ages, when it was called the Bank Croft, a common with rights of pasture. A later map from the Records Office (see Walk 5) shows where two canal basins were dug in 1816. The larger one was eventually filled in. When you tackle Walk 14 to Wilmcote, a notice on the wall of the canal cottage by lock 40 will tell you (among other things) that although the canal was authorised in 1793, it was not opened through to the River Avon until 1816. The present gardens were laid out in the 1930s (Charles Edward Flower would have been appropriately impressed).

Finally, spur left then right, towards the road bridge (number 69) over the canal. The World of Shakespeare is on the far side (looked at in Walk 3). Two pedestrian crossings return you to the TIC.

Walk 3: Central Stratford (3)

Route: As Walk 2 to Holy Trinity churchyard – Old Town – Church Street – south end of Chapel Street – Chapel Lane – Waterside: crossing to bridge 69 – TIC; pedestrian crossing in Bridge Street – TIC.

Start: The TIC in Bridgefoot.

What you will see: Hall's Croft; Mason Croft; The Almshouses; The King Edward VI Grammar School; The Guild Chapel; The site of New Place and Nash's House; The Great Garden of New Place; The World of Shakespeare.

The Walk

Leaving the churchyard of Holy Trinity Church (see Walk 2), instead of going right, into the gardens, continue ahead along Old Town. Cross the entrance to Southern Lane with some care. You will pass several sixteenth century houses: The Dower House, next-door to which is Avoncroft, and a gap of five metres brings you to timber-framed Old Town Croft, which is opposite the entrance to College Street. Facing another Guide Friday stop is:

Hall's Croft

This sixteenth century, timber-framed house was, by all accounts, the home of Dr John Hall and Susanna Shakespeare (the elder daughter of the Bard) during the early years of their marriage. The leaflet describes what you will see, for example, the paintings in the parlour, the Tudor and Jacobean furnishings, and a dispensary fitted out as it would have appeared in

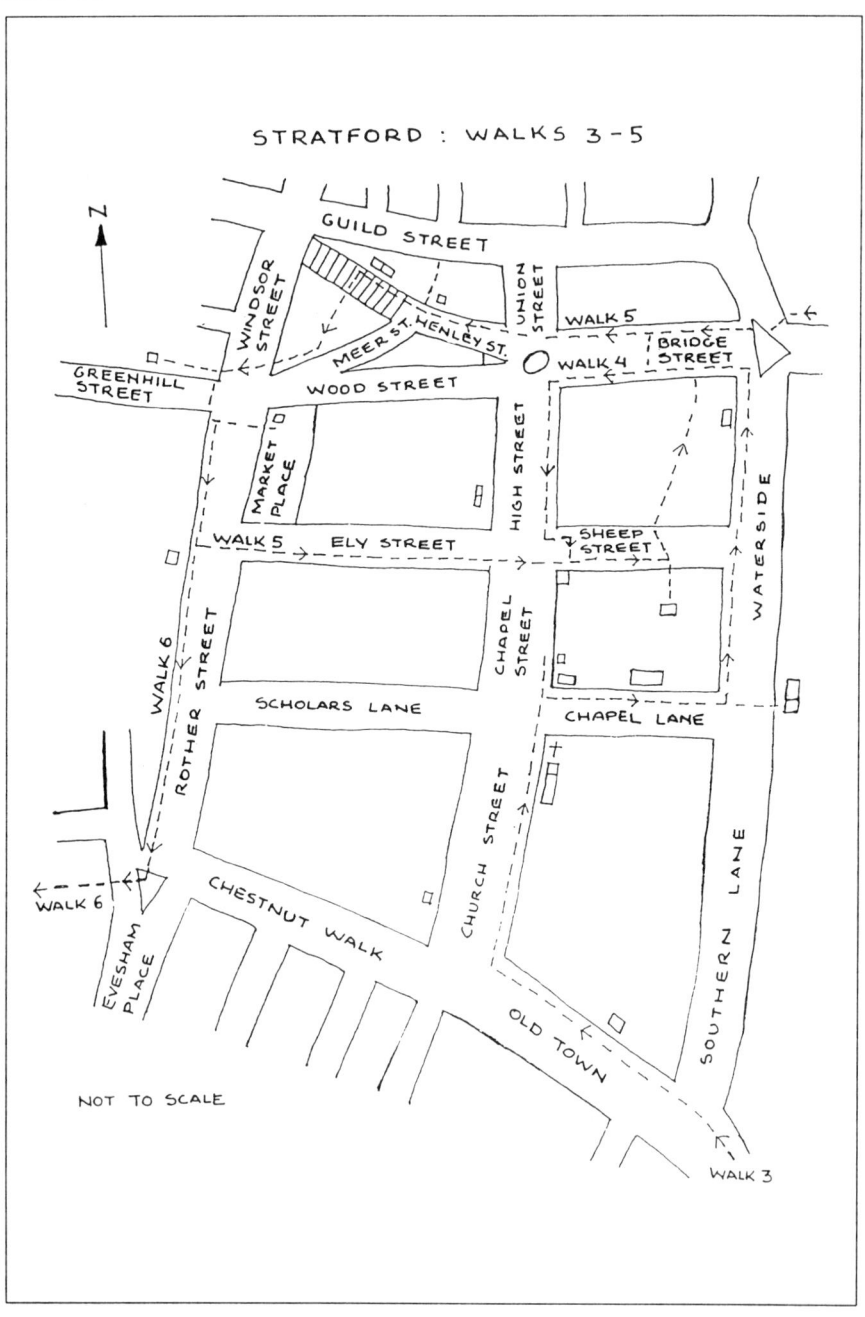

the first Elizabethan age. Dating the dates: they married in 1607, living here until William Shakespeare's death (1616), when they moved to New Place. Dr Hall died in 1635; Susanna in 1649. You may have already seen their gravestones in the chancel of Holy Trinity Church during Walk 2.

Emerging, go right, then right along Church Street. Walking north-east, pass the Windmill Inn, and on the other side you will see:

Mason Croft

Built of relatively new eighteenth century brick, and during the early part of this century, the home of Marie Corelli, a popular and flamboyant novelist of her day. It is now occupied by the Shakespeare Institute of Birmingham University.

Later, on this right-hand side:

The Almshouses

A paced fifty metres of timber-framed housing, built around 1427, and extended and restored in subsequent years. There is a notice on the wall (hunt about to find it): '... built by The Guild of The Holy Cross ... to provide homes for aged local people, and this use is continued down to the present time ...' All mod cons now, though.

Then follows:

The King Edward VI School

A notice hangs in the (private) entrance: 'These buildings ... created by the Guild of The Holy Cross in the fifteenth century ... confiscated by King Edward VI who later restored the school to the town ...'

The building dates from 1417. The Guild Hall (on the ground

The Almshouses and tower of the Guild Chapel

floor) was the HQ of the Guild of the Holy Cross until Henry VIII's Reformation. The upper floor, called the Over Hall, was where, in all probabilty, the Bard received his education. Full of old desks (names carved in), today; in Elizabethan schoolrooms, pupils usually sat on benches, books perched on their knees. This education, for sons of burgesses, was free but. on a chauvinistic note was for boys only. By custom, girls stayed at home with their mothers.

At the corner of Church Street and Chapel Lane stands:

The Guild Chapel

As with Walk 2's Holy Trinity Church, for walkers, a browsing is irresistible. Additionally, you should find a leaflet inside which more than adequately describes the Guild of the Holy Cross and chapel.

Briefly: the Guild itself was established before 1269, the year that the chapel was first completed. The nave and tower were rebuilt in the 1490s. Then came Henry VIII's Reformation: from the mid-sixteenth century, the monasteries were dissolved and much church wealth confiscated. The Guild of the Holy Cross was no exception, the chapel losing its rood loft and screen, its wall paintings whitewashed, many to be lost forever. As described in the leaflet, the chapel, certainly one of the buildings familiar to William Shakespeare (ministering to the Grammar School), was granted by the Crown to the Bailiff and Corporation of Stratford (see the subsequent window read). The leaflet also describes the Doom Painting above the chancel arch (soon to be viewed from below), telling you that it dates from shortly after 1500.

Looking up at the battlemented, pinnacled tower, a golden rooster silently crows on high. Pinnacles and battlements line the sides of the chapel. At the north porch, gargoyles stare down – the one on the left is pulling a particularly ugly face. Services are held: 'Wednesday 10am, Saturday 12 noon (April-September and the first Saturday of every month)'. The chapel is closed during the two days of the Mop, when the fair descends; and when, unless on a dodgem, you will not be able to drive through the centre of the town.

Inside, the organ is to the right (sometimes played as you wander). Beyond the eighteenth century font, on the south wall, you may be lucky enough to find the previously mentioned leaflet. Money for this and other contributions goes in the slot in the wall, by the door. Near the leaflets are the Chapel and the Doom Painting (see below) as they used to be.

The nave was rebuilt by Hugh Clopton. His tomb chest is in the Clopton Chapel of Holy Trinity Church (see Walk 2), though he was buried in St Margaret's, Lothbury, London.

Walking east along the tiled nave, above the chancel arch,

is what's left of the Doom Painting: Christ with the Virgin and St John at the top; Hell on the right, and a built-up Heaven with St Peter on the left.

Entering the chancel – through stained glass, darkly – there is much reading material at the base of several of the windows to supplement the leaflet. For example: 'A chapel was first built here in 1269 for the brethren and sisters of the Guild of the Holy Cross and was enlarged and reconsecrated in the fifteenth century. On the suppression of the Guild in 1547, the chapel passed to the ownership of the Mayor, Aldermen and Burgesses of Stratford.'

Returning along the nave, you will discover more scraps of paintings on the west wall, some of which are hidden by panelling.

Incidentally, the leaflet includes a form for application for membership to become a Friend of the Guild Chapel (open to any interested person), its purpose being the chapel's preservation and use. Seems like a good idea. No leaflets? Try Nash's House.

Standing once more at the entrance of the north porch, think holy thoughts and smile up at the left-hand gargoyle, next crossing to the south corner of Chapel Street with much care to:

The Site of New Place and Nash's House

The house, New Place, was built by Hugh Clopton at the end of the fifteenth century and bought by the Bard in May of 1597. He did not live there permanently until 1610. It was here, on 25th March, 1616 (in his fifty-first year), that William Shakespeare signed his will, witnessed by the lawyer, Francis Collins. He left New Place to his daughter Susanna. After his death on 23rd April, 1616, Susanna moved to New Place with her

Nash's House

husband Dr John Hall. The house was later occupied by Susanna's daughter, Elizabeth, and Elizabeth's first husband, Thomas Nash (married 1626), and second husband, John Barnard (married 1628). William Shakespeare's 'line' ended with Elizabeth in 1670. New Place was eventually rebuilt by another Clopton, Sir John, and finally bought, then pulled down by the Reverend Francis Gastrell in 1759. By all accounts, the good cleric engaged in combat with a certain mulberry tree, whose leafy descendants will soon be seen in The Great Garden of New Place.

Next-door, still in Chapel Street, is Nash's House (New Place Museum), which also permits entry to the site and gardens of New Place. As ever, the leaflet is a good buy.

With origins in the early seventeenth century, Nash's House belonged to Thomas Nash, Elizabeth's (first) husband. The leaflet describes the sixteenth and seventeenth century furnishings that you will see within the property. Among the portraits are several deemed to be of Elizabeth and Thomas Nash, and Elizabeth and John Barnard. The upstairs museum records the history of Stratford from prehistoric times through to the eighteenth century. As with Susanna and Dr Hall, you may have already seen the gravestone of Thomas Nash in the chancel of Holy Trinity Church when walking Walk 2.

Budding horticulturists may wander around a Knot Garden. This consists of four beds in formal Elizabethan mode with shrubs, herbs and flowers, many of which relate to Shakespeare's days.

One may now move from the Knot Garden directly into another (see below), or first return to the corner, by the site of New Place, and go left along Chapel Lane. Opposite the entrance to the Grammar School, you come to:

The Great Garden of New Place

Enter, bearing right – much evidence of topiary – to your left, the mulberries, the smaller tree: '... planted by Dame Peggy Ashcroft on 8 September 1969 to commemorate the 200th anniversary of the first Shakespeare festival ... organized by David Garrick in 1769,' and the sprawling, older tree, surrounded by a dry-stone wall: 'Morus Nigra ... a scion of the tree planted by Shakespeare ...'

Emerge into Chapel Lane, continuing left to the theatres. At the T-junction, go left along Waterside, passing the entrance to Sheep Street. Barnaby's Fish Restaurant is on the corner. Further, you should see a notice on the wall: 'Flood water levels – January 1st 1901 – May 23rd 1932.' Happy ducks, unhappy walkers; waders required then. A few metres beyond there are public toilets and:

The World of Shakespeare

Hi-tech Bard which, according to a leaflet, recreates during '25 action-packed minutes ... the authentic atmosphere of Elizabethan England.' Bear-baiting, the plague cellar and the Royal fireworks are featured. There is a Puppet Masters Workshop; also a Studio Theatre and Costumes Exhibition.

Finally: either cut across the road with care to bridge 69, the two pedestrian crossings and the TIC; or bear left to Bridge Street's pedestrian crossing by W.H. Smith, crossing and going right, back to base.

Walk 4: Central Stratford (4)

Route: TIC – two pedestrian crossings – Bridge Street – pedestrian crossing – High Street – north end of Chapel Street – Sheep Street – Shrieve's Walk – pedestrian crossing in Bridge Street – TIC.

Start: The TIC in Bridgefoot.

What you will see: Harvard House; The Garrick Inn; The Town Hall; The Armour Museum (Arbour Antiques).

The Walk

NOTE: please refer to the map with Walk 3

From the TIC, retrace the route taken in Walk 1 to the road bridge over the canal, going left over the first pedestrian crossing (as ever, keeping a wary eye open for traffic) to the traffic island; then ahead, this time, to another pedestrian crossing, a Belisha-beaconed zebra, and the start of Bridge Street.

On the right there is a forest of bus stops, where one may get on or off the Stratford Blue (and elsewhere in the town) when part-walking the country walks. See the Travel Guide.

Continue as far as the two-stage pedestrian crossing, crossing with care to the other side of Bridge Street, by W.H. Smith, then bearing right a few metres and going left into High Street. Nearing the end of this street, you may wish to brave the traffic for a closer look at:

Harvard House

Timber-framed, furnished in the Elizabethan style and rebuilt by Thomas Rogers in 1596 (there were two fires in the town in 1594 and 1595). Katharine, the daughter of Thomas and Anne, married Robert Harvard, whose son, John, emigrated to the good old US of A to eventually endow Harvard University.

Adjacent and offering refreshment, stands:

The Garrick Inn

Also dating from the late sixteenth century, and named after David Garrick (1717-1779), the British actor and theatre manager. He is remembered for his Shakespearean performances as Richard III, Hamlet and King Lear, for example. Walkers of Walk 3 will recall the 'mulberried' festival reference in the Great Garden of New Place.

Recrossing, another signpost points to the many places of interest. Situated on the opposite corner (of Chapel and Sheep Streets) stands:

The Town Hall

Built in 1767, on the Sheep Street side, there is a statue of the Bard donated by David Garrick; on the Chapel Street side, in patriotic block capitals, the words: 'GOD SAVE THE KING'. George III succeeded his grandfather, George II, in 1760.

Now turn into Sheep Street; walking along, you should see a couple of signs: 'Antiques Arms & Armour', following, bearing right, to:

Arbour Antiques

Browse, admire and buy – a leaflet is available describing the History Craft range of gifts (clocks, sporting etc) and Guest Products (ceramics, handicrafts etc). It is worth the visit just to look at the armour that is on display.

Shrieve's House

Cross Sheep Street and continue your walk; there are several timber-framed houses that date from around 1600. On this side, a building known as the Shrieve's House (No. 40) particularly catches the eye. By this house, a cobbled strip tempts the shopper – the 'Abode' of gift ideas. Still on a Shrieve's theme, a few metres east of number 40, you will see a signed Shrieve's Walk. Window-shopping and emerging, once more, in Bridge Street. Now, it is a simple matter of retracing your steps, left, to the pedestrian crossing by W.H. Smith; cross the road and go right, back to the TIC.

Walk 5: Central Stratford (5)

Route: TIC — two pedestrian crossings — Bridge Street — Henley Street — path to Meer Street — Greenhill Street — Market Place — Rother Street: a) Ely Street — Sheep Street, joining Walk 4; b) Continue along Rother Street, starting Walk 6 to Anne Hathaway's Cottage at Shottery.

Start: The TIC in Bridgefoot.

What you will see: The former Market House; The Public Library; Shakespeare's Birthplace; The Teddy Bear Museum; The American Fountain; Mason's Court.

The Walk

NOTE: please refer to the map with Walk 3

As with Walk 4, from the TIC, proceed to the road bridge over the canal, going left over the first pedestrian crossing to the traffic island and then ahead to the striped zebra, and the start of Bridge Street.

Continue along the right-hand pavement — a busy street, this, overflowing with cars and people in the summer. At the roundabout, cross the entrance of Union Street with some care to, oddly, two more timber-framed buildings which are still part of Bridge Street, and where Henley Street begins.

Opposite stands a white building, now a bank, which was the former:

Market House

The Market House was built in 1821. Above, there is a white

turret with a greenish, copper dome, topped off with a weathervane. Get your bearings and the lie of the wind.

Sailing into Henley Street, pass the new Post Office. On the far side, there is yet another Shakespeare reminder – the aptly-named shopping arcade, Bard's Walk. Further, on the right, you come to:

The Public Library

Timber and books: part of the library dates from the early sixteenth century. The creaking stairs inside lead to a Local Studies Area.

A path at this corner would take you (bearing left at Guild Street) to:

The Records Office

This is the local history study centre for Stratford and its surrounds: crammed with books, old maps, photographs and so forth. It is open to anyone – just sign in: the helpful and knowledgeable staff will answer any queries that you may have.

From the point of view of this walk, proceed along Henley Street, a welcome pedestrianised section, passing Hornby Cottage and Shakespeare's Birthplace to:

The Shakespeare Centre

Built in 1964, the Centre is the headquarters of the Shakespeare Birthplace Trust which manages the Shakespearean properties. Devoted to the Bard, with a comprehensive collection of books and theatrical archives, and available to academics and non-academics (me, the latter); as with the Records Office, just sign in. A telephone number is 01789 204016.

Shakespeare's Birthplace

The sixteenth century, timber-framed house that everyone comes to see; and where, in all probability, William Shakespeare was born a day or two before his baptism in Holy Trinity Church on 26th April, 1564. Originally two houses – western and eastern – the Bard is thought to have first seen the light of day in the western half. In 1857/58, the property was restored to a drawing of 1769, and adjacent housing demolished.

Entry to the Birthplace is via the Centre. Briefly: the tour starts with a Visitors' Centre, then passes through a garden to the Birthplace 'proper', comprising: ground floor rooms, exhibition room, upstairs rooms (one of these is the 'birthroom'

Shakespeare's Birthplace

with its seventeenth century cradle and glass-cut names), rear wing and kitchen. The furnishings throughout are appropriate to Shakespeare's time. More garden brings you to a shop – Hornby Cottage (once lived in by Thomas Hornby, a blacksmith), and part bricked over during the early nineteenth century. As ever, the leaflet is a good buy; any queries, just ask the staff within.

Family Tree

William Shakespeare's father, John Shakespeare, was the son of Richard Shakespeare who farmed as a tenant on land in Snitterfield (the land was owned by Robert Arden of Wilmcote). Mary Arden, John's wife-to-be, was Robert Arden's eighth and youngest daughter from his first marriage. John Shakespeare moved to Stratford from Snitterfield some time before 1552. He is on record (hardly improving the air quality of the neighbourhood) as being fined for making a dunghill ('sterquinarium') in Henley Street in that year. John Shakespeare was a glover by trade, though he also dealt in barley, timber and wool, for example. He did not sign his name, 'making his mark' at times in the shape of a pair of glover's dividers. Fortunately for theatre-goers, in 1557 (or thereabouts), John Shakespeare married Mary Arden, quite possibly in Aston Cantlow's Church of St John the Baptist (see Walk 15). William Shakespeare was their third child and first-born son.

Continuing with the walk, facing (nearly) the Centre is the sign: 'The Minories Shopping Mall'. Go along here to Meer Street.

Bear right to the right-hand pavement, the Market Place is opposite (open-air market on Fridays), using the pedestrian crossing across the start of Windsor Street to reach Greenhill Street. A matter of metres to, on your right:

The Teddy Bear Museum:

Hundreds of teddies: Paddington, Rupert and Winnie the Pooh in the Teddy Bear Hall of Fame; the Teddy Bears' Picnic, library and Victorian dolls house. A leaflet from the TIC is available. Ring 01789 293160 for a free mail-order catalogue.

Back at the start of Greenhill Street, take the pedestrian crossing to the opposing side. The Old Thatch Tavern is on the corner. Temptingly, further along Greenhill Street, not far from the lights, is the Greenhill Fish Bar. At this corner, another pedestrian crossing brings you to the Market Place and:

The American Fountain

The fountain dates from 1887 and was dedicated by the actor Henry Irving (the stage name of John Brodribb). He was the first actor to be knighted, staging many Shakespearean productions, including Romeo and Juliet, with himself and Ellen Terry in the lead roles. No 'fountaining' water, nowadays: 'The gift of an American citizen, George W. Childs of Philadelphia to the town of Shakespeare in the Jubilee Year of Queen Victoria.' 1887 was Queen Victoria's Golden Jubilee Year.

With safety in mind, recross, then go left along the right-hand pavement of Rother Street, passing the Herald offices and the Civic Hall (another TIC in here). Further, just beyond the Christadelphian Hall, you come to:

Mason's Court

I first thought of the word 'quaint' to describe this building, but this is not quite right. Quaint as in old-fashioned rather than bizarre, perhaps. The building is extremely easy on the eye – fifteenth century, timber-framed, with a tiled roof.

Walk 5: Central Stratford (5)

The American Fountain

'Wonky-looking', as though about to tilt over at any moment, though it will still be standing in another five hundred years.

Opposite – music for walkers – is Symphony Cottage. Here, one may return via Ely Street, the entrance of which faces the Christadelphian Hall, passing another fish and chip shop, then moving ahead into Sheep Street, joining Walk 4. Alternatively, continue along Rother Street, making for Anne Hathaway's Cottage at Shottery, as described in Walk 6.

Walk 6: Shottery – Anne Hathaway's Cottage

Route: As Walk 5 to Rother Street – Evesham Place – path to/from Shottery – Evesham Place – Chestnut Walk – Church Street, joining Walk 3.

Distance/Terrain: From Evesham Place, an easy, level fifteen minutes, one-way.

Start: The TIC in Bridgefoot.

Parking: For those who decide to drive and visit separately, a (paying) car park is to the left, as you face Anne Hathaway's Cottage.

Public Transport: Anne Hathaway's Cottage lies alongside the Guide Friday route (the stop is in an adjacent coach park). There is also a stop at Evesham Place. The route is from the TIC, through the town (stopping at Evesham Place), then on to Shottery; from there, the bus continues to Wilmcote and back to Stratford (not the other way). Additionally, the local bus stops in Cottage Lane on its way back to town. Details are in the Travel Guide and the Guide Friday leaflet.

Refreshments: As well as in Anne Hathaway's Cottage (between spring and autumn), edibles are available further to the right – The Cottage Tea Garden and The Thatch Restaurant.

Toilets: Again, within Anne Hathaway's Cottage, but you will have to pay to get in and use them.

What you will see: Anne Hathaway's Cottage.

50 *Exploring Stratford-upon-Avon*

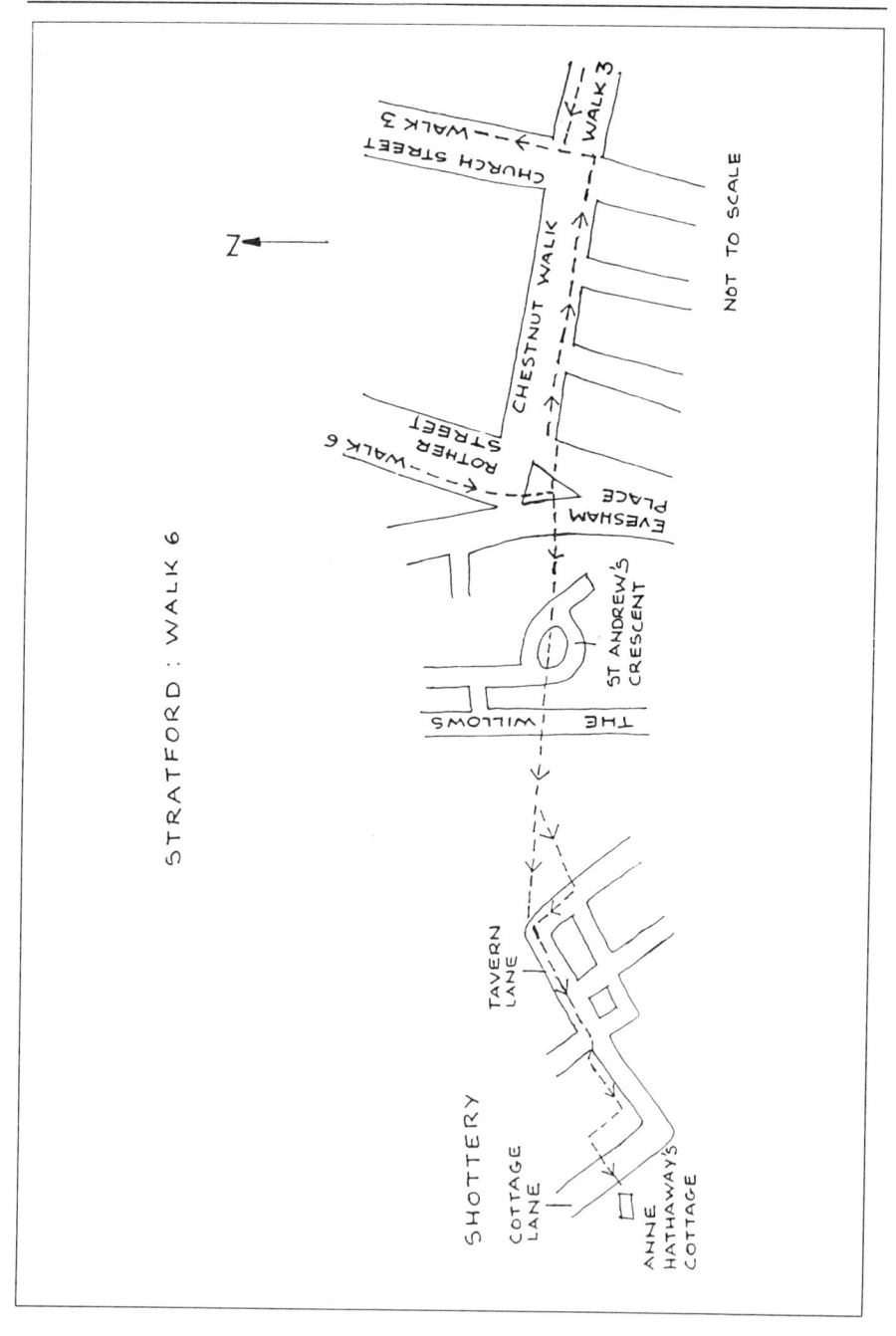

The Walk

Extending Walk 5, wend your way along the right-hand pavement of Rother Street, eventually coming to the small garden where Rother Street and Grove Road meet, and Evesham Place. Cross with care to the triangular traffic island. Taking the pedestrian crossing on your right, then going right a few metres, will bring you to the start of a path to Shottery and Anne Hathaway's Cottage. Woodstock Guest House is on the corner.

An Elizabethan arrow points the way to a tarmac path, moving straight across St Andrew's Crescent, clearly crescent-shaped, and along a path between the fencing of back gardens, soon crossing The Willows. Further, the path opens onto Shottery Fields. Continue ahead, west-north-west, give or take a degree, ignoring the left-hand path part of the way along.

You come to a signed fork and path choice: left for Shottery; right for Tavern Lane. Here, I offer (optimistically) the best of both worlds, the left fork with a detour via Tavern Lane, as well. Bearing left, a healthy-looking crop of leeks on one side (eaten by the time you get here), and going ahead where the tarmac ends – semi-surfaced – to the main road. A sign directs to Anne Hathaway's Cottage.

Now follows the scenic route as you turn right, north, along Tavern Lane, passing several attractive timber-framed houses, thatched and tiled, on to the bend in the road by Bramley House. Follow the road as it curves left (west) to the main road, continuing ahead by way of the right-hand pavement as far as the mini-roundabout. Cross and climb the steps to the right of the entrance of Cottage Lane. A kissing-gate leads to the start of Jubilee Walk, as defined by the tablet on the right commemorating the Silver Jubilee of Queen Elizabeth II. This walk is mentioned in the soon-to-be-purchased leaflet. Onward along the path around to the right, alongside Shottery Brook, then over the footbridge to the road and purpose of the walk:

Anne Hathaway's Cottage

Even from the pavement, the house is an eye-catcher: thatched, timber-framed and packed with bricks. A panel at the entrance gives some detail. The leaflet gives much more.

Formerly a farmhouse, the lower part is fifteenth century; the western end dates from around 1600. This was the home of Anne Hathaway who (as nearly everyone knows), married the Bard. A-wooing he would go, walking here from Stratford, perhaps even taking this route; perhaps not.

The leaflet describes what you will see, for example: the Cottage Garden, the rooms in the property (including furniture that belonged to the Hathaway family, particularly a sixteenth century oak bed complete with rush mattress in one of the bedrooms), the Orchard and Shakespeare Tree Garden. Many of the flowers, herbs, shrubs and trees relate to Shakespeare's time. Any queries, just ask the staff within.

Marriage and Children

There is no record of the marriage of William Shakespeare and Anne Hathaway. However, there is an entry dated 27th November, 1582, in the register of the Bishop of Worcester for the granting of a special marriage licence (that avoided the normal triple calling of the banns) between William Shakespeare and Anne Whateley of Temple Grafton (a village about 7 miles to the west of Stratford). The Whateley instead of Hathaway is assumed to be a clerical error; this is supported by record of a bond being taken out on the 28th November, which 'absolved' the Bishop of responsibility for any irregularities concerning the marriage of William Shakespeare and Anne Hathaway.

Anne Hathaway's Cottage

They may have married at Temple Grafton or Stratford; no one really knows. Anne's gravestone in Holy Trinity Church records that she died on 6th August, 1623, aged 67; struggling with the arithmetic, she was born in 1555 or 1556, and was eight years older than husband, William. So, they were married at the end of November, 1582, and the registry of Holy Trinity Church records the baptism of Susanna six months later on 26th May, 1583. Twins Hamnet and Judith were christened on 2nd February, 1585.

Once more on the pavement: refer to Public Transport if you decide to catch the bus back; best of all – retrace your steps for another fifteen minutes of healthy exercise!

Standing by the Elizabethan arrow in Evesham Place, maybe, recross the first pedestrian crossing to the triangular traffic island, and then take the second pedestrian crossing to the far side of Evesham Place. Finally, by going left a few metres, and right, along Chestnut Walk, one may (crossing with care), turn left into Church Street, joining Walk 3.

Walk 7: Environs (1)

Route: TIC – start of Clopton Bridge – riverside path – Fisherman's Car Park – TIC.

Distance/Terrain: Walk 6 with water – an easy, level twenty minutes, one-way.

Start: The TIC in Bridgefoot.

Refreshments: Within the town.

Public Toilets: The multistorey Bridgefoot.

The Walk

This is a very short and simple affair – pass to the left of the TIC to Bridgeway, and left along the pavement; Bridgefoot's multistorey car park with its toilets, is nearby. Proceed as far as the pedestrian crossing. The Moat House International is on the far side. Take this pedestrian crossing; further to your left is the Leisure Centre, exercising those parts that even a walk will not reach. There are swimming and teaching pools, squash courts, a health suite (sunbeds, gym and sauna), even a fitness assessment; outside, there are synthetic grass courts. The Centre also offers refreshments and has toilets. One would join here if parked at Riverside.

Bear right, pavementing roughly south, and at the corner of the Moat House, go left along the tarmac path, due south, in the distance, you can see the diminutive toll-house of Clopton Bridge (described in Walk 1). Ignore the left-hand path half way along, continuing to the road for a road's width look at the toll-house which dates from 1814.

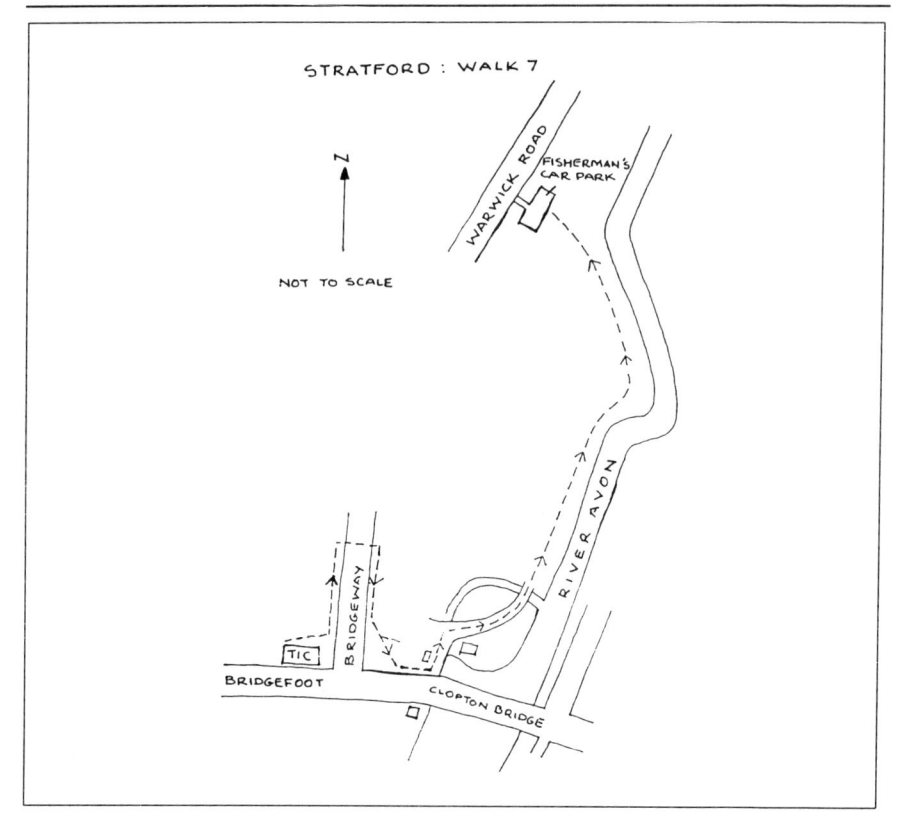

Turn left a few metres, then left again, down the steps. Stratford Marina Ltd is on your left, water on your right. Further, bear right, walking roughly east, arching a concrete footbridge over the water. It is tarmac all the way, now, as you advance, north-east, fairly close to the River Avon – amazingly easy, level walking.

Later, a notice warns about unauthorised fishing. Walking along here one day, one fisherman commented, despairingly: 'There are more fish in my aquarium than in this (expletive deleted) river!' Yet I have seen good catches in the keepnets lifted from the Avon near the recreation ground. I did not dare to tell him, of course.

Stratford Swans

The views on this side of the river are not so good; those on the far side are better – detached housing with gardens reaching down to the water's edge; several narrow boats are moored. And then the last stretch – on the opposite bank willows weep attractively and sheep nibble, hungrily.

Eventually, the path curves around to the Fisherman's Car Park, which is the end of the walk, though it is possible to continue along the bank for a short distance. There are facilities for boats but no public toilets. Incidentally, one may drive via the A439 and park here; it is signed Warwick Road Car Park. There is a panel map of the area, and a metal plate set in brick: '... path constructed by Community Programme workers ... October 1985 – October 1986.'

And then back again – a new walk: everything looks different going the other way, even a luckless fisherman, hooked on worms.

Weir across the River Avon

Walk 8: Environs (2)

Route: Footbridge – South Avon path – Avon/Stour bridge – South Avon path – track past Milcote Manor Farm and Milcote Hall Farm – pavement alongside the B4632 – path to Seven Meadows Road – footbridge.

Distance: About 6 miles.

Maps: O.S. Landranger 151. O.S. Pathfinder 997.

Start: By the footbridge over the Avon, near the Seven Meadows road bridge, on the south side of the river.

Terrain: A touch of mud. Stiles to be climbed. One or two minor ascents/descents.

Refreshments: Within the town and mentioned *en route*.

Public Toilets: As for Refreshments.

The Walk

From the footbridge, go under the road bridge to a gate clothed in arrow-heads. You will return via the path on the left. Through the gate and on by the River Avon where fishermen fish, hopefully, holding rods about a mile long. Further, the river passes either side of an island. On the far side, a weir; on this side, a lock. The path to be taken wends to your left, an arrow-head directs; but first, why not go ahead a short distance for a closer look at the lock? There are seats for sitting and treed views to be enjoyed. A notice on the island describes the: 'Weir Brake or Anonymous Lock'.

Continuing with the walk, there is a fairly short, stepped ascent; it levels out with a wooden handrail, then heads down

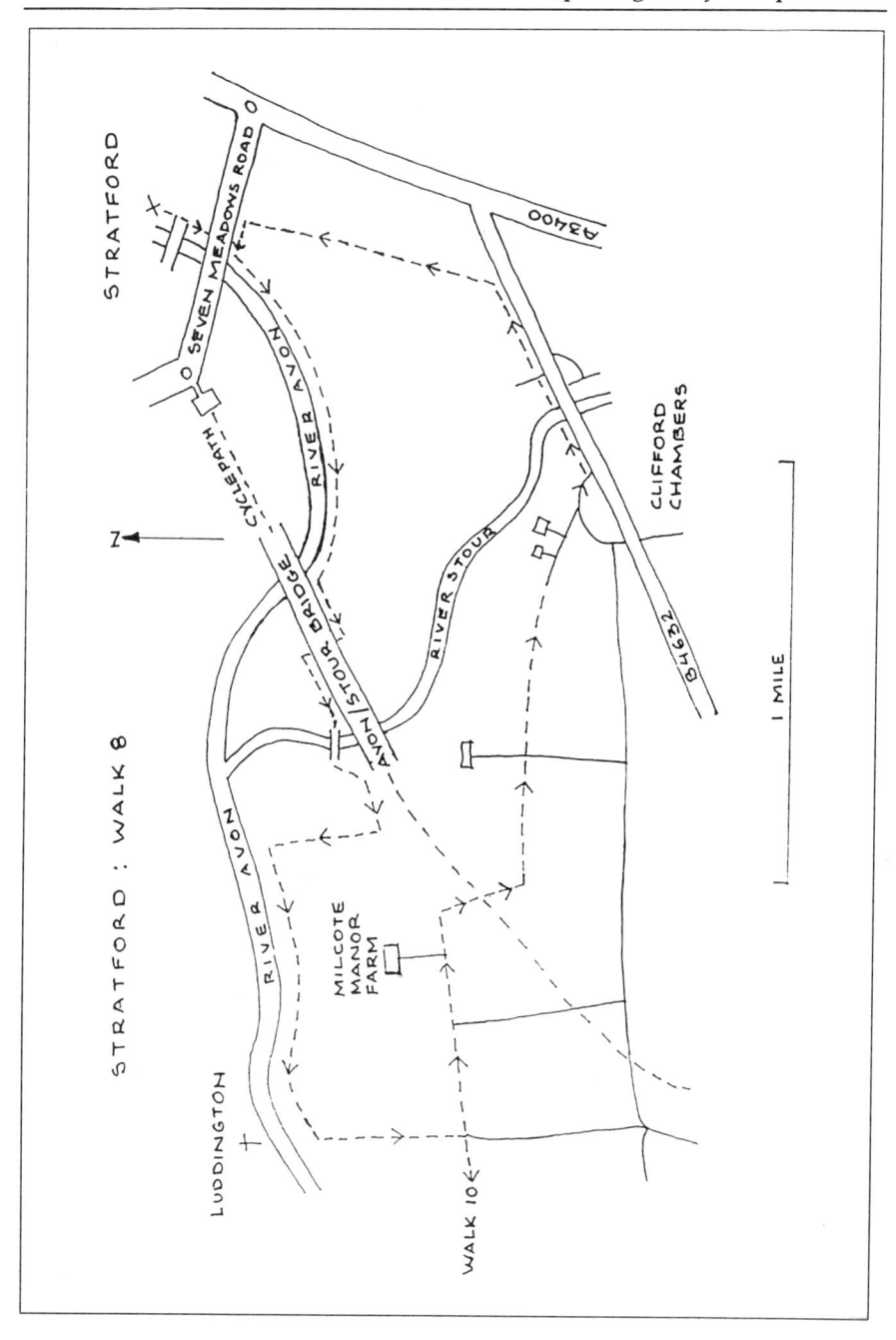

a flight of steps and continues. Later, more steps curve away to the right; in the wetter months, this is a muddy and not entirely easy descent.

Onward, scaling the stile, you come finally to a field. Bear right, walking in a westerly direction along the right-hand edge. Continue through a second field, currently freshly ploughed and in the sun, good to look at, but not walk on; fortunately, there is a grass strip on this side. Into a third field, with the Avon now close by; beyond the far bank, you should see the North Avon path and cyclepath. The latter crosses the Avon/Stour bridge (the old railway bridge) which should also be visible in the foreground.

Several paths criss-cross the area and this one is no exception. Continue past the Avon section of the bridge to a wooden gate; pass through this and go along a fourth field, to a stile on your right, which leads up to the cyclepath. But you go ahead a few metres and right, north, under the 'square' bridge, then immediately left, west, towards the River Stour. At the bank, bear right, taking the 'piped' footbridge over the river, next turning left, yet not following the Stour under another 'square' bridge, moving roughly south-west, away from the water, as indicated by the yellow arrow-heads.

As ever, onward, walking a 'tad' south of west along the edge of a field, the fence and cyclepath to your left. As I walked this stretch, spring was being sprung – lush, green grass and ruminating cattle. But whatever the season, go right at the far left-hand corner and bear left over the stile and footbridge, along the River Avon's south bank. A succession of fields, stiles and footbridges, passing Milcote Manor Farm, a weir (Walk 9's Luddington is opposite), soon strolling south, away from the Avon, coming to a post and narrow metal road. A yellow arrow-head points the way you have just come. A blue arrow-head points right, along a grassy track (see Walk 10).

Turn left, east, along the road – easy, level walking, past Milcote Manor Farm's south side, and making a right angle by housing where the road becomes an unsurfaced lane. Cross the cyclepath, keeping to the main route. Turn sharp left, east, again, eventually passing the entrance to Milcote Hall Farm with tarmac underfoot, to a short section of road off the B4632. On the right is a road signed to Weston and Welford, two villages which are the focus of Walk 10. Opposite, is Clifford Chambers, looked at in Walk 11.

You could, if you wish, move ahead three walks, entering Clifford Chambers. But from the point of view of this walk, turn left along the pavement, initially north-east, joining the B4632. Make progress over the Stour Bridge, with warning notices: '... private fishing – warning – baliff and guard dog patrolling ...' On the other side stands the refurbished Clifford Mill. Just beyond, is a signed footpath, Clifford ¾, which would take you to the Shire Horse Centre, also looked at in Walk 11. Further, you pass the road entrance to the SHC. According to the notice, it has an English Shire Restaurant, and toilets, too. Feel free to detour for a quick cuppa.

About a hundred metres past the bridge, you come to a stile on your left. Up and over, walking roughly north, across and then along the edge of a field, negotiating a small wooden gate. Soon, you see the tower and spire of Holy Trinity Church in the distance as you descend. The bridge over the Avon hoves into view: part of Seven Meadows Road, which used to carry a railway line. Sad to relate, but there are many ex-railway lines in the Stratford area, victim of the Beeching axe. At least the track beds are useful for walking and the banks often provide a home for wildlife. You come, at long last, to a path that 'parallels' Seven Meadows Road. Turn left, back to the South Avon path and the previously-mentioned gate clothed in arrow-heads. A final right, under the road bridge, returns you to the footbridge over the Avon, and the start of the walk.

Walk 9: Luddington

Route: Footbridge – Greenway – cyclepath – Avon/Stour bridge – North Avon path – Luddington – Avon/Stour bridge – South Avon path – footbridge.

Distance: Up to 5 miles.

Maps: O.S. Landranger 151. O.S. Pathfinder 997.

Start: By the footbridge over the Avon, near the Seven Meadows road bridge, on the south side of the river.

Terrain: Muddy in places, with numerous stiles.

Public Transport: Bus 218 between Luddington and Stratford, Mondays to Saturdays. See the Travel Guide.

Refreshments: Within the town.

Public Toilets: Within the town.

What you will see: The lock, weir and Church of All Saints at Luddington.

The Walk

Cross the footbridge and go left, along the tarmac path, initially south-south-west, soon veering right, north-west, as shown by the sign: 'The Greenway', walking parallel to Seven Meadows Road. Continue ahead into the small car park, which fills up very early; hence the preferred use of Bridgefoot and Riverside. If you want to risk it, several of the walks pass through here, the car park is accessed via Seven Meadows Road.

The panels on the right-hand side are worth a read: one tells you about The Greenway and has a useful map of the area; a second describes Stratford's former railway junction. As you can see, there used to be a network of lines in the area; one such, the former track bed, now the about-to-be-walked cyclepath, is hard and level, and will take a pushchair or wheelchair.

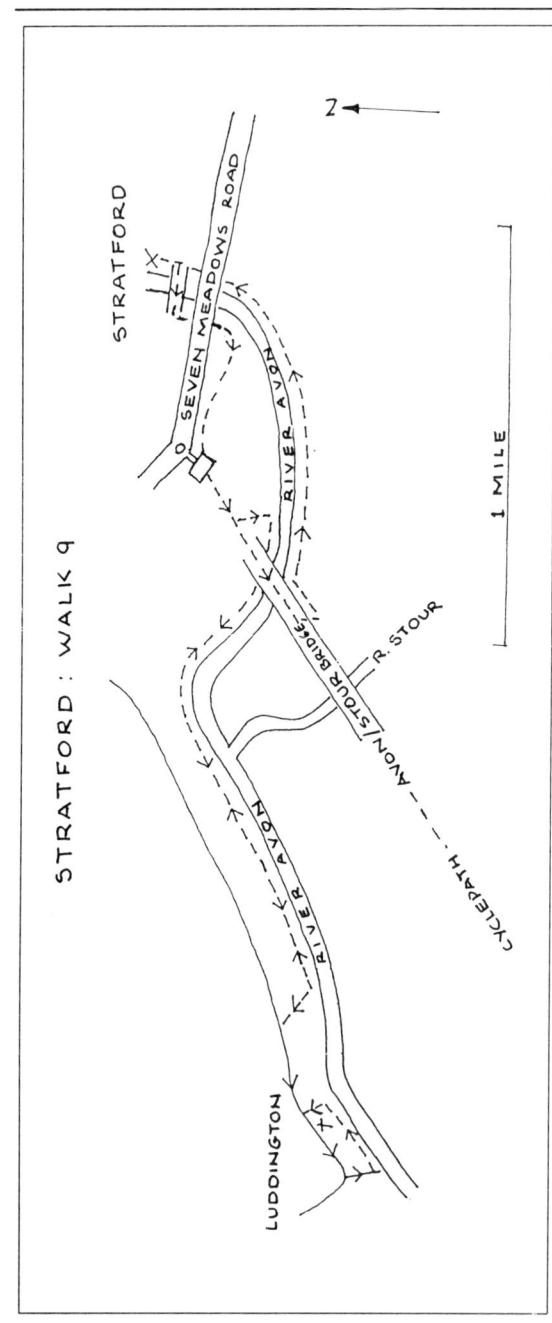

Continue past the panels and along the cyclepath, roughly south-west. Three paths combine to some wooden fencing. Weave through and on. A notice defines the 'Cyclepath to Milcote picnic area' walk. On your right is the racecourse. Tracking the track bed, another notice asks cyclists to ring their bell when approaching walkers – watch out for them – and 'bell-less' joggers, too.

Walk 9: Luddington

The Lock at Luddington

Approaching the Avon/Stour bridge (the old railway bridge), take the path on your left down to the river bank with seats and tables for picnickers. Bear right and go under the arch closest to the river, footsteps echoing, following the path, west, to fencing, an arrow-head and a stile. Go up and over to a field, continuing west alongside the Avon, veering north, backing west, crossing a footbridge, walking between two close-cropped hawthorn hedges. Ignore the right-hand path near the pumping station as you advance by the river.

This is a winding and sometimes muddy route, so watch where you walk, up and down steps and along – you can see where the Stour meets the Avon. Next comes a stretch of back garden walking, strong on scenery and gates (to be closed), with the occasional dog, and even a scampering squirrel.

The path leaves the gardens for a long field, still close to the river, negotiating a 'piped' footbridge, sundry stiles and much grass. Further, just before a line of trees, bear right, north-west, up to a stile in the fence. Scale, making for the diagonally opposite corner of the field, where yet another stile brings you to the road and Luddington.

Turn left along the verge, moving through the village, crossing with care to a patch of grass and an attractive thatched house close to Boddington Farm. There is a modicum of pavement here and there, but do keep an eye open for traffic. Pass the telephone box on the other side (you will emerge nearby, shortly), more thatched housing, and a reminder to keep your walking speed to 30 mph.

Where the road curves sharply to the right, cross cautiously, taking the stile by the gate and then along the unsurfaced lane, direction south, to the lock and weir over the Avon. This is a good place to wander and enjoy the view. There is a high-arched footbridge over the centre of the lock, from which to look down at the boats and rushing water.

Return a short distance to a circular, concrete rubbish bin, bearing right, walking close to where the boats are moored, and just past a seat to: 'Eric Pritchard 1923-1984 Navigator and Craftsman', go left to the stile and along. Luddington's Church of All Saints is only a stone's throw away and may be visited. The leaflet describes an earlier chapel, a Shakespearean legend, and the building and fabric of the present nineteenth century church. Climb the stile next to a gate, turning left, emerging onto the road beside the telephone box. The bus [see Public Transport] stops, opposite, on its way back to Stratford. There is a timetable on this side, and another seat on which to wait.

Needing more exercise? Retrace back to the Avon/Stour bridge, passing under the same arch and up to the cyclepath. Bear left, crossing the Avon, continuing for about 70 metres, taking the path on your left, down to a stile. Scale this stile: Walk 8 tracks right, under the 'square' bridge but this walk strikes immediately left, roughly east, along the South Avon path, repeating the first part of Walk 8, in reverse. Briefly: short section of field 1 – gate – field 2 – gate – field 3 – an arrowed gate into field 4. Further, go left, by way of an unsigned path – Walk 8's sometimes muddy mix of stepped ascents and descents, eventually descending to the lock and weir. Why not sit awhile? Swans dip their elegant necks, in between, hoping for a handout from yours truly. Continue along the river bank towards Stratford, under the road bridge and back to the footbridge, the start of the walk.

Walk 10: Welford-on-Avon and Weston-on-Avon

Route: Footbridge – North Avon path – Avon/Stour bridge – cyclepath to near Milcote Manor Farm – track to Weston: a) Retrace from Weston, as below; b) Paths to Welford – retrace to Weston – track to near Milcote Manor Farm – cyclepath – Greenway – footbridge.

Distance: Up to 8 miles.

Maps: O.S. Landranger 151. O.S. Pathfinder 997.

Start: By the footbridge over the Avon, near the Seven Meadows road bridge, on the south side of the river.

Terrain: Virtually level all the way. Muddy mud in the winter.

Public Transport: Bus 218 between Welford and Stratford (also passes through Luddington), Mondays to Saturdays. See the Travel Guide.

Refreshments: Mentioned *en route* in Welford.

Toilets: Pubs in Welford.

What you will see: A brief description of All Saints Church, Weston is given.

The Walk

Foot the footbridge – up, across and down – then bear left, south-south-west, along the tarmac path. Where the path curves right, by the sign: 'The Greenway', go ahead, along the North Avon path, banking the river, edging the field. Walk south-west, passing the weir with its compressed rapids – it's surprising how the tempo of the river changes, only metres and the water is almost becalmed.

Scale the stile and on, direction west, by way of the grassy path, taking in your stride a 'part-piped' footbridge and wooden footbridge. To your left, beyond the river, the South Avon path; to your right, the cyclepath; with you in the middle, converging on the Avon/Stour bridge.

Approaching the bridge – Walk 9's seats and tables are still there – bear right up to the cyclepath, then go left to cross the Avon. A long, level stretch of track bed is solid underfoot. Lettering etched in seats tells you that Stratford is 2 then $2\frac{1}{2}$ miles away, to where the cyclepath is crossed by an unsurfaced lane. There used to be a milk halt here, serving the surrounding farms.

Turning left would enable you to join Walk 8 on its way east and north, back to Stratford. This walk turns right, north-west to south-west, by housing, where the tarmac begins. As ever, onward, passing the entrance to Milcote Manor Farm and ignoring the road on your left. The tarmac fades, slightly, acquiring a central grass strip and the occasional pothole. Away to the right, you should see the spiky spire of Luddington's church, passed close by in Walk 9. Further (much) where the main route curves left, a yellow arrow-head on a post points right (walkers of Walk 8 emerge here). You follow the direction of the blue arrow-head, the equine option, ahead, initially west, taking to the grass. Approaching the housing, you reach the bungalow, Corna Brae, and continue as far as All Saints Church, Weston-on-Avon.

Walking along the path towards the south porch of this fifteenth century church with bordering roses, a Senecio and some Bergenias, then looking up at the battlemented tower and part-battlemented south side, and a gargoyle or two. First, a

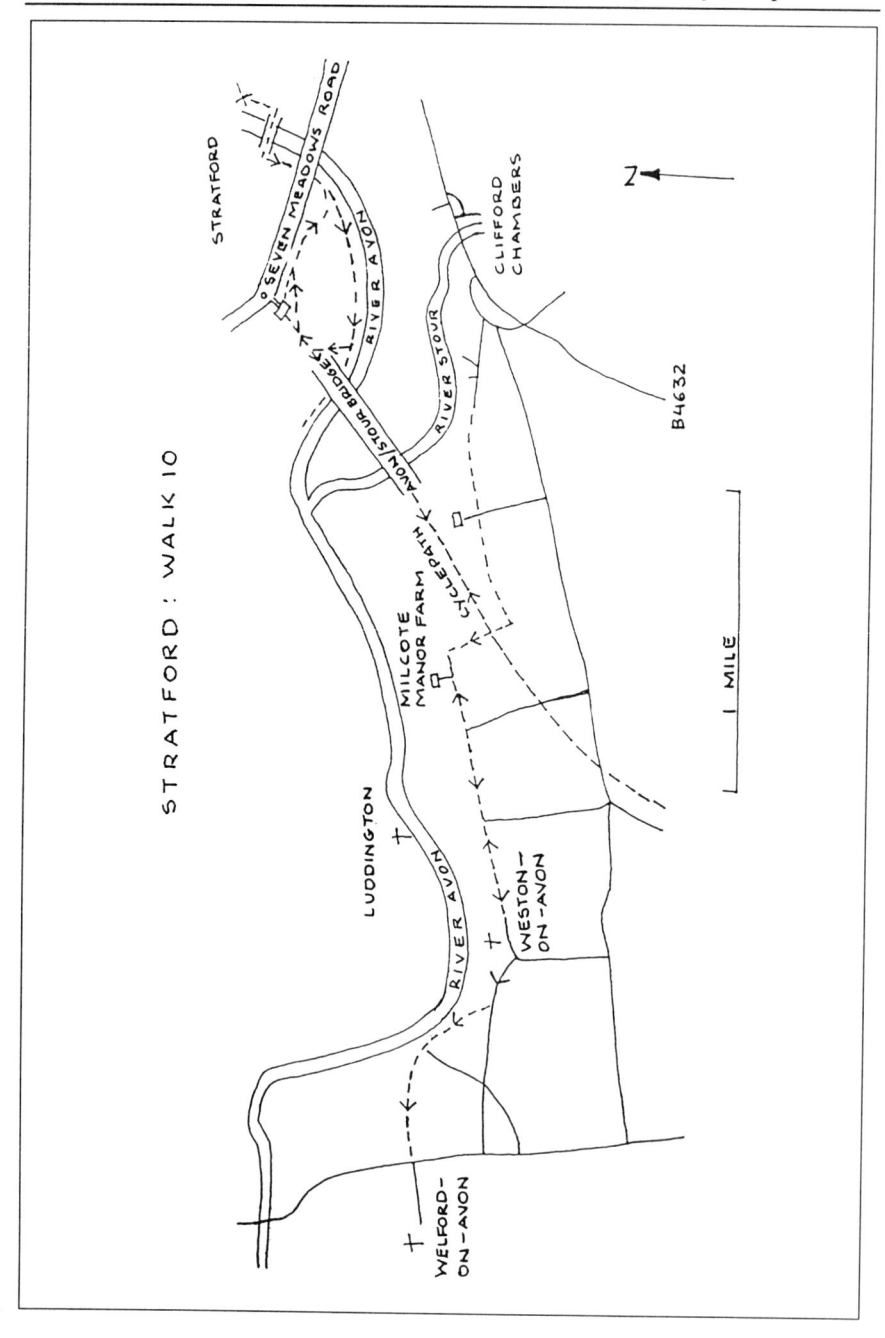

All Saints Church, Weston-on-Avon

tour of the outside: going right, in the south wall there is a 'squint', permitting a view of the altar (mind the Bergenias), and around to the north side, also battlemented.

Entering the porch, you will in all probability find that the door is locked and you will have to trek to Threeways, the white house on the corner, opposite, for the key. They may not be in, but persevere, going left along the road to Weston Farm (farm shop beside) until you track down the key. And what a key – a huge chunk of metal – insert upside down and turn clockwise to open the door.

Inside, a notice on the south wall tells you that a history of All Saints may be purchased. If they have sold out, you could, of course, make do with second best, this brief description – though still putting your money in the slot in the wall.

Moving east down the nave, approaching the chancel arch, the tiles surrounding the wooden pulpit are medieval. On the north side stands a seventeenth century bier. Further, to the right of the altar, is a brass to Sir Edward Grevill (1559); and to the left, another to Sir John Grevill (1546). Walking west – a squint through the squint from within – go back along the nave and leave the church. It goes without saying (though I am about to) that you have locked the door and returned the key.

Now, you may either retrace your steps (described later) or continue to Welford, as follows:

At the corner, by Threeways, go ahead and to the right slightly, north-west, along the road. You will see several thatched houses, strong on eye-appeal, as you progress to a post weighed down with arrow-heads. Turn right, north, soon strolling quite close to the Avon, passing Pear Tree Close (a house) and Witch Gate (a witch on a broomstick), and at this corner, bearing right, as indicated by the arrow-heads. Continue with tarmac then grass underfoot, finally threading

Walk 10: Welford-on-Avon and Weston-on-Avon

between two houses (the one on the left is thatched and timber-framed) to High Street and Welford-on-Avon.

Conveniently, opposite, is a seat, on which to wait for the bus back to Stratford [see Public Transport]. Crossing and going ahead along Church Street will take you to the Church of St Peter. To the right, the Bell Inn for a liquid top-up, and the Post Office (nuts, chocolate and inedible stamps).

Welford is an attractive village and repays a wander – up, down and around, particularly to the right, towards the river.

Options: getting the Stratford Blue or retracing your steps through Weston, along the cyclepath near Milcote Manor Farm; this time, following it across the Avon/Stour bridge to the Greenway, then bearing right, on to the first footbridge and start of the walk.

A couple of alternatives to Weston are possible, but it is easy to lose your way. The route is currently unsigned in places where new housing is going up. I will point you to the start and leave the rest to you.

At High Street (seat opposite), cross to the pavement and turn left, south, keeping a pedestrian eye on the far side. The first alternative starts by the telephone box where a sign points to Fraser's Way and Miller's Close, and has a white walker on a blue background, as well. Alternative Two continues further along High Street, going left into Chapel Street, passing The Shakespeare, the Wesleyan Chapel and weaving a vague route back to Weston. Once started, keeping mainly east should get you there. I prefer the retrace; everything really does look different the other way.

Walk 11: Clifford Chambers

Route: TIC – two pedestrian crossings – Tramway Bridge – Tramway Path – Kipling Road – Loxley path – right fork south of Heath Farm to the A3400 – Clifford Chambers – pavement alongside the B4632, joining Walk 8 – footbridge – TIC.

Distance: Up to 5 miles.

Maps: O.S. Landranger 151. O.S. Pathfinders 997 and 998.

Start: The TIC in Bridgefoot.

Terrain: Level, with plenty of mud in the winter. Innumerable stiles. Several busy roads to be crossed with care.

Public Transport: Bus 215/6 between Clifford Chambers and Stratford, Mondays to Saturdays. There is a bus stop and shelter near the New Inn. Refer to the Travel Guide if you intend to bus it back to town.

Refreshments: The New Inn in Clifford Chambers offers food, wet and hoppy draught Bass, a wood-burning stove (welcome in the winter) and Spanish swords above the bar. See, also, The Shire Horse Centre.

Toilets: Pubs and in the SHC.

What you will see: A brief description of the Church of St Helen's is given; The Shire Horse Centre.

The Walk

From the TIC, proceed to the far side of the Tramway Bridge as described in Walk 1. Cross the road, going ahead along the Tramway Path. Stratford Butterfly Farm (see Walk 1) is on the left. Onward, south, and just before the end of the recreation

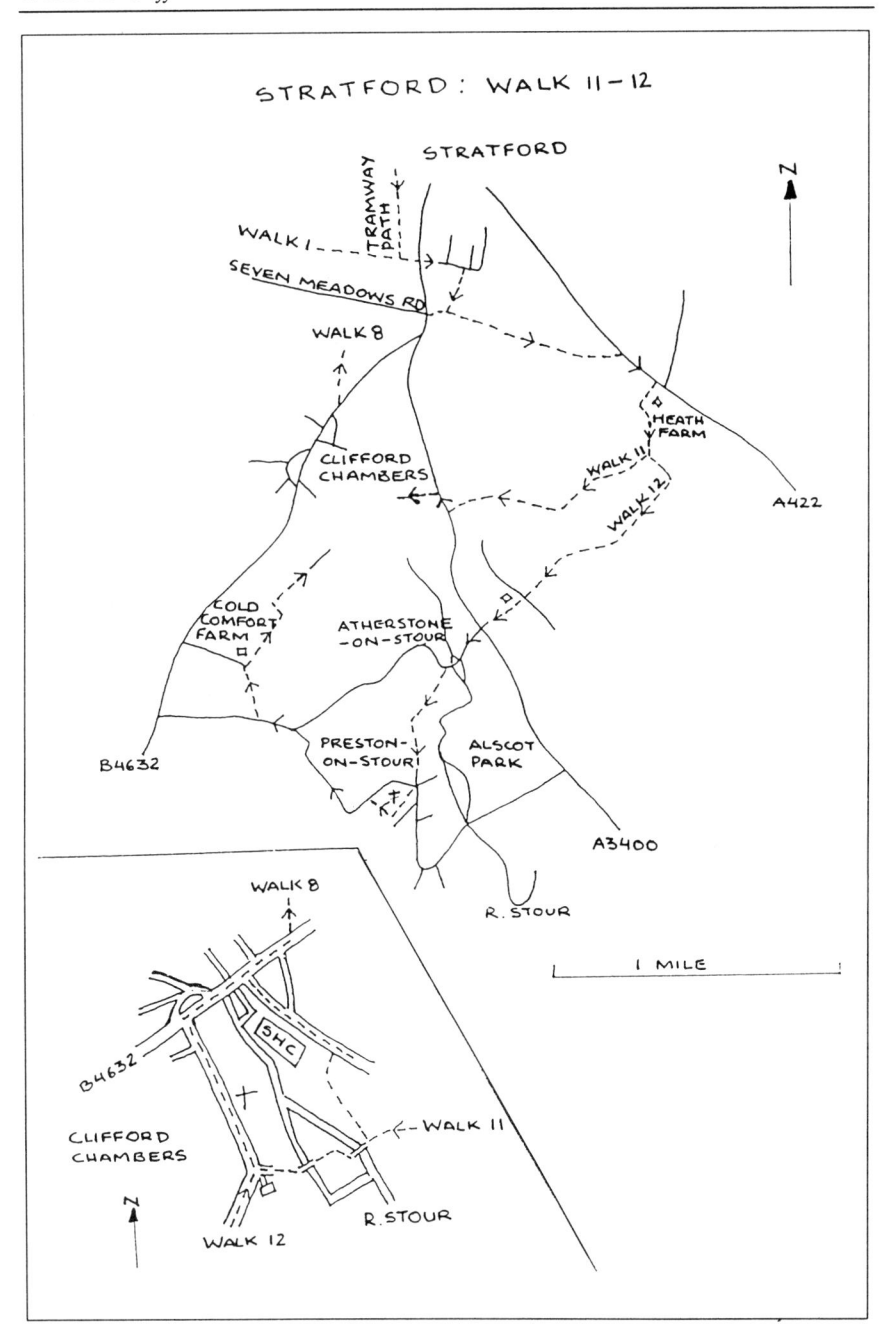

Walk 11: Clifford Chambers

ground, bear right, off the path, descending and then turning left, under the arch to the A3400. Cross with care, taking the path opposite and to the right, slightly, between housing with lamps for night walkers – to the curve of Kipling Road.

Continue ahead on the left-hand pavement, passing Tennyson Road – the street names are on a poet theme – the estate is known as The Poets. Further, you come to a stile in fencing on your right, and the notice: 'Private land please keep to the rights of way.' Over and along, south-west, to a point about 100 metres from the track bed (privately owned and not for walkers). The path splits in two: going right, west, will take you to the hoardings, roundabout and start of Seven Meadows Road; but you bear left, east, joining the path to Loxley.

It is only a matter of metres to a stile – go over, walking along the left-hand edge of the field. Scale the stile into a second field, at the end of which you go through a gap in the hedge to your left, to an unsurfaced lane. Next, move to the right, following the lane, resuming an easterly direction. Further, where the lane curves right to a farm, continue ahead, through another gap to what is now a fourth field. A fifth field brings you to the A422.

Cross with much care to the narrow pavement opposite. The path to Loxley, only three miles away, wends east. You turn right – a confined five minutes' of pavement – and just before the road to Tiddington, recross to the entrance of Heath Farm: the start of a signed path to Ailstone, with a notice at one side asking you to keep dogs on a lead and fasten gates.

Take this path, south-west, passing to the right of Heath Farm. On through the first gate, leaving the 'cobbly' lane for grass, going ahead, an arrow-head on a post directs to a second gate. There is a stile beside the gate, and possibly an old bath. Here, strike south across the field, making for the diagonally opposite corner, coming eventually to a last gate and pair of arrow-heads.

One points left, south-east, towards Hines House Farm (to be followed in Walk 12). Beyond the gate, bear right, south-west, keeping the field's fence to your right, soon crossing the track bed. Again, arrow-heads direct west – currently, a crop is growing and the route is unclear; an abundance of mud, though. You are aiming, now, for a line of trees, and a stile. Weave between the wood and blackberry bushes to another stile. The remainder of this section consists of a succession of fields and stiles, forever west, to the A3400.

Turn right, along the right-hand pavement of what is an often busy road – ninety measured paces – crossing to a 'gas pumping station'. You can see where the gas pipeline was laid. Pass to the right of the Colditz fencing, following the arrowed path to a stile, along fields one and two, to the start of field three. You may see a stile standing in splendid isolation to the left, where a hedge used to be. Continue ahead for twenty metres or so, then bearing right, north-west, to the bridge over Stour One.

At the start of the bridge, one may continue north-west to the Shire Horse Centre, which I will describe later, after a look at the church.

Cross the bridge and on over Stour Two, to the road and Clifford Chambers. The Old Mill is on the left. A new house, newly timbered and thatched, is on the right-hand corner. You would approach via the lane to the south-west if walking Walk 12.

Further on the left is the Manor House, which dates from around 1700. Brasses to the Rainsford family, Lords of the Manor in times past, may be viewed in the church. The church booklet, to be purchased shortly, tells of a community of monks – read all about it.

Go north-west along the main street of this attractive village, passing the sixteenth century, timber-framed rectory to the Church of St Helen's.

Originally Anglo-Saxon, the church was rebuilt in Norman times. A major restoration took place at the end of the nineteenth century. Walking through the churchyard, noting the battlemented, pinnacled tower, with a wafer-thin rooster on top, and into the south porch. The door arch is Norman. There is a mass dial scratched in the stone above.

Enter the church and, on the table, the aforementioned booklet is available for a few pence; an interesting read. On the left, the font with seven sides of chunky stone; unquestionably Saxon work, according to the booklet. The arch of the blocked door in the north wall is also Norman.

Looking in the direction of the tower, there is the wooden screen: '... in loving memory of Graham and Kathleen Rees-Mogg ...', and above, a glass superscreen: '... in ever loving memory of James Robertson Black churchwarden of this church for 35 years ...' The booklet tells of an ancient bier under the tower presented to the church by John Shakespeare.

Walking east along the nave, approaching the chancel, on your left is a Jacobean pulpit with the sort of wood you want to run your hands over.

At the end of the choir, on the north wall, are the Rainsford brasses (no rubbing allowed according to a note on the choir stall): '... Rainsford ... Lord of the Manor of Clifford who married Elizabeth Parry ... 1583 ...' Also another brass to a lady, higher up to the right. On the north wall of the sanctuary, you will see a finely carved and decorated monument to the Rainsford family. The stained glass of the east window catches the eye. Near the south-east corner is a Norman pillar piscina, and on the south wall, a tablet to: '... John Parry Nash (surgeon) ...' (1816).

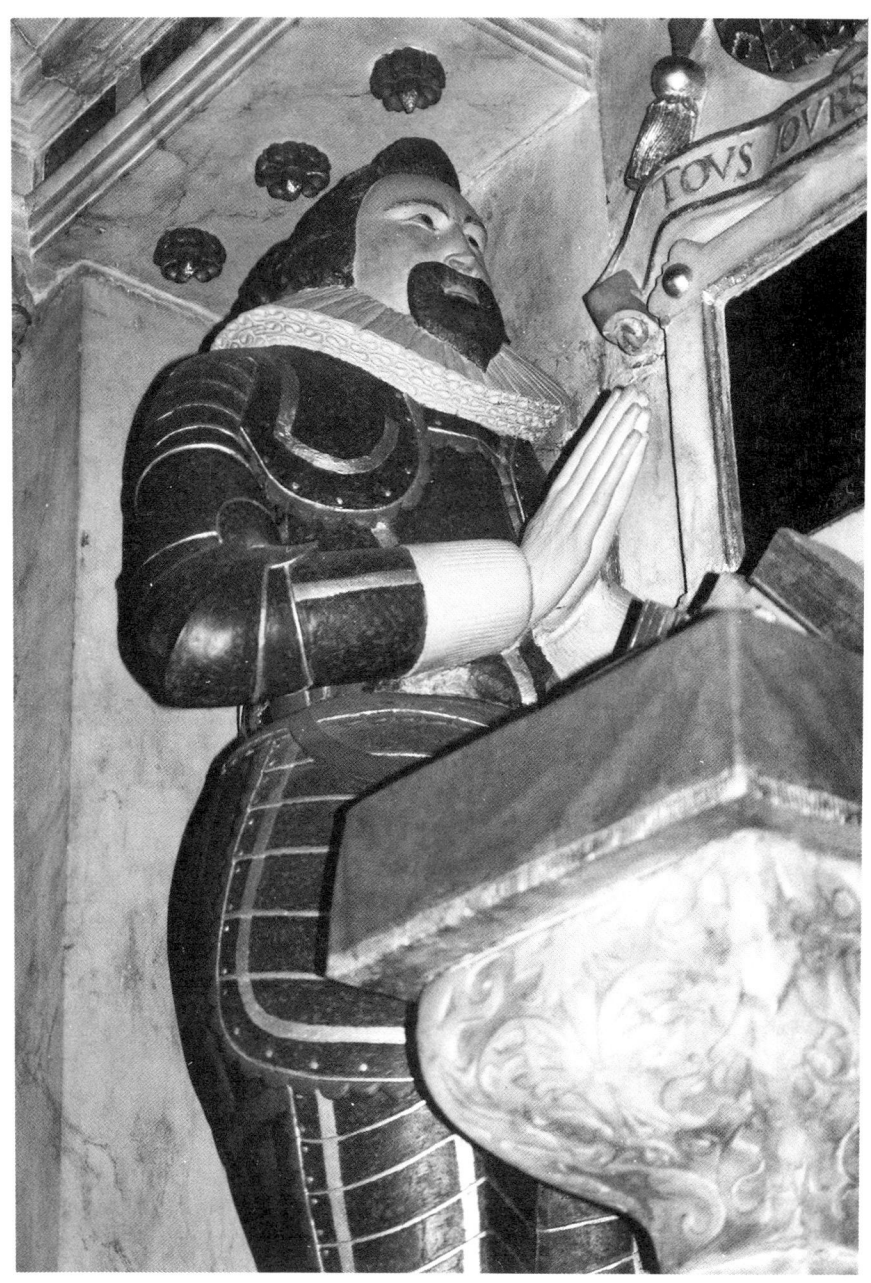

Monument to the Rainsford family (detail), church of St Helen, Clifford Chambers

Back at the road, you can, if you wish, go right, along to the New Inn and bus stop, and proceed as described later, or retrace to the start of the bridge over Stour One for a look around the Shire Horse Centre, as follows:

Facing the bridge, go right, north-west, across the field – on through the gate into a second field with a high-stepping stile at the end. In this third field, climb the stile by the gate, half-way along the right-hand hedge. Walking north-east, a Trojan Horse may be seen to the left as you leave the grass for a track and come to a junction. Bear left, past a tethered dog to:

The Shire Horse Centre

See the shire horses, 'hooty' owls, falconry displays; take a wagon ride. A selection from a programme which can vary according to the time of year. There is a licensed restaurant and snack bar. For armoured walkers, medieval banquets are held on Friday evenings (booking essential), offering musicians, entertainers, food and wine, the edibles being served by 'richly costumed maidens'. Appetite whetted, ring them on 01789 266276 for a crusading experience. There is plenty of free parking if you want to drive and visit separately; certainly if banqueting. A leaflet is available from the TIC.

Leaving the Centre, you have a choice: retrace to and through Clifford Chambers via the bridges, or go left, north-west, along the concrete-to-tarmac lane to the B4632. Taking the latter, a sign, Clifford ¾, points the way you have just come.

More options: next to this sign, cross (with extreme care) to the opposite pavement, going right, joining Walk 8 on its way back to Stratford; or bear left for a few minutes' of grass verge then cross the Stour, ignoring a possibly diverted path on your left, and turn left into Clifford Chambers.

Standing, finally, at the north-west end of the village, near the New Inn [see Refreshments] and bus stop [see Public Transport], either catch the bus to Stratford or retrace to the B4632, joining Walk 8.

Walk 12: Preston-on-Stour

Route: As Walk 11 to south of Heath Farm – left fork to the A3400 – Atherstone – Preston – Clifford Chambers, joining Walk 11.

Distance: Up to 7 miles.

Maps: O.S. Landranger 151. O.S. Pathfinders 997 and 998.

Start: The TIC in Bridgefoot.

Terrain: Level with wintry mud. Stiles aplenty. One negligible ascent near Cold Comfort Farm. Busy roads to be crossed with care.

Public Transport: Bus 50 between Preston and Stratford, Mondays to Saturdays. See the Travel Guide and the Preston crossroads reference during the walk.

Refreshments: The PO/stores in Preston for DIY snacks. Refer, also, to Walk 11 in Clifford Chambers.

Toilets: None in Preston, but see Walk 11.

What you will see: Alscot Park in passing; A brief description of the Church of St Mary in Preston is given.

The Walk

NOTE: please refer to the map for Walk 11.

The walk is identical to Walk 11 as far as the fork, south of Heath Farm. So, with a minor repeat, having passed by Heath Farm and struck south across the field, make for the diagonally opposite corner, the last gate and pair of arrow-heads. One points right, south-west, the route taken by Walk 11. You take the other, towards Hines House Farm, walking in a south-easterly direction, keeping the fence/hedge to your left as it curves right, south, veering south-west, eventually crossing the track bed.

Climb the stile on the far side, taking care with the steps and possibly slippery sleepers over the ditch. Proceed south-west across the field to an arrow-head on a post and the tarmac. Pausing for a mud decoke, maybe, bear left, south, following the tarmac around to the right, south to west, semi-surfaced; further, going ahead, away from Ailstone Farm, to a stile. Over and along, with the wire fence to your right – walking the wide open spaces – don't forget the waterproof if there is even the slightest chance of rain. Leave the fence where it angles right, for another stile, then head left, roughly south, staying fairly close to the left-hand fence – a sizeable stride – to yet another stile in the opposing fence. Next, comes, at the time of writing, a spot of coniferous walking (perhaps given the chop by the time you get here).

There is no clear view of the way ahead; go fractionally south of west, as indicated by the arrow-head. Two more stiles and a field bring you to a metalled lane. Pass to the left of the warehouse, along a tree-arrowed path, over a patch of rough ground, to the A3400.

Cross with some care, taking the road signed Atherstone-on-Stour. From within a garden, a dog barks and wags – friend or foe, I wonder – advancing over the Stour to where the road bends right towards what was once Atherstone's church. St Mary's was, however, declared redundant and sold in the summer of 1994; not easily converted to a home, I would have thought. The tower and spire may be visible between the trees and can be seen from a distance later on.

At this point, leave the road, moving to the left of a timbered, thatched house (lucky horseshoes in the wood above the door), following the path south-west. Further to your left, you will see the battlements and tall chimneys of stately Alscot Park – beautifully furnished inside, by all accounts, but not open to the public. In the mid-eighteenth century, the estate was owned by one James West, Secretary to the Treasury. He financed the rebuilding of St Mary's in Preston-on-Stour (to be visited).

Stay with the main route, south – not bearing right over the concrete footbridge – walking along the left-hand edge of the field, taking the left-hand gate (arrow-head on post), carefully avoiding the 'freshly-heaped' molehills dotted around the faint outline of the path, while at the same time enjoying the excellent views of the meandering Stour and Alscot Park. Finally, go through the wooden kissing-gate, to where the road begins, entering Preston-on-Stour.

One soon runs out of adjectives when describing villages in the Stratford area; Preston is certainly deserving of a wander.

Housing, Preston-on-Stour

Before continuing, I should mention that the main street, south, will take you past the PO/stores (local honey and sticky stamps for sale) and Coronation Hall to the crossroads, where you may get a bus back to Stratford (a few stop in the village) [see Public Transport].

Still some way from the War Memorial, bear right (south-south-west) across the grass, passing a fine old timber-framed house. The three decorative gables are certainly in keeping with the character of the village. The brick house to its left has unusual wooden cross windows. The church has a wooden cross on its north wall, and a lot more; so on to the gates (not easy to open) and Church of St Mary.

If you walk around the churchyard walk you can see the pinnacles that line the walls; there is one at each corner of the battlemented tower; the yews go back a few years, as well.

Access is via the door in the west wall of the tower. Inside, on the north wall hangs a Mappa Mundi. A second door reveals a Visitors' Book and 'slot' for contributions; feel free. There is no booklet to be purchased, but there are framed notes, also on the north wall. They will tell you that the church was rebuilt between 1752 and 1757 (for James West, as previously mentioned), that the tower is fifteenth century, and that most of the glass in the west window dates from the fourteenth to sixteenth centuries.

Standing by the font – looking back up at the gallery – one may see the Royal Arms of the Stuarts and four hatchments, and on the walls below: well-executed kneeler patterns.

Walking east along the nave: on the north wall, a tablet with the words 'In memoriam General Sir Michael Montgomerie Alston-Roberts-West G.C.B. D.S.O. 1905-1978', and above, a wooden Christ on the Cross, and a banner. On the south side: The Creed, Ten Commandments and Lord's Prayer. Now is a good time to look back and admire the colouring of the stained glass of the west window.

In the chancel, the east window, of predominantly seventeenth century glass, catches the eye. Monuments and tablets are everywhere, in particular, one to Sir Nicholas Kempe (1624) and his two wives, Cicelie and Sarah. Read the detail at the base.

Leaving the church, do not, unless you have decided to return by bus, retrace your steps through the churchyard, but take the gates opposite, west of the tower, bearing right, north-west, along a grassy track to the road. Turn left, passing a 'risk of grounding' warning (for lorries, not walkers) – and continue beyond a second grounding notice. Where the road curves sharply right, north-east, bear left, west, leaving the road for a track. After about ten metres, turn right, north-west, before a house, advancing to just past the trees, where stands a stile on the right.

Scale, for a change, proceeding north across the field. At the opposing hedge, close to a 'mini-arrow-head' on a telegraph pole, go around the fence into another field, walking north-north-west, the fence to your left, approaching Cold Comfort Farm. Keep to the left-hand side of the same field, veering right, north-east, ascending, levelling and, at the end, moving into the adjacent field. Follow the line of the path, soon passing to the right of the trees. A white arrow-head on a green disc should point the way you have just come. Execute a swift left and right where the trees end, resuming a north-easterly direction, eventually going right a few metres and ahead along a lane, entering Clifford Chambers.

Walkers of Walk 11 will recognise the Manor House on the right, and the newly timbered and thatched house on the far corner. Accordingly, catch the bus or stroll back to Stratford, as described in Walk 11.

Walk 13: Snitterfield

Route: TIC – canal path – Welcombe Road – Welcombe Hill Obelisk – optional circular route around Snitterfield – Welcombe Hill Obelisk – TIC.

Distance: Up to 6 miles.

Maps: O.S. Landranger 151. O.S. Pathfinders 997 and 998.

Start: The TIC in Bridgefoot.

Terrain: Mostly level, with a minor ascent or two approaching the Welcombe Hill Obelisk. A generous helping of mud in the winter, especially when negotiating the section from Snitterfield to the Obelisk. Boots are recommended. One busy road, the A46, to be crossed with care.

Public Transport: Bus X16 brings express relief to weary walkers, passing through Snitterfield on its way from Coventry to Stratford. See the Travel Guide.

Refreshments: The Foxhunter and Snitterfield Arms in Snitterfield. The latter offers a tasty selection of 'home-cooked' food: walking a circle, you might consider trying the ring sausage (a speciality of the house). 'Wings of Fire' and 'Death by Chocolate' look interesting.

Toilets: Pubs

What you will see: The Welcombe Hill Obelisk; A brief description of the Church of St James the Great in Snitterfield is given; a church with Shakespearean associations.

The Walk

From the TIC, walk roughly west, past the Pen and Parchment and entrance to Bancroft Place, keeping to the right-hand side

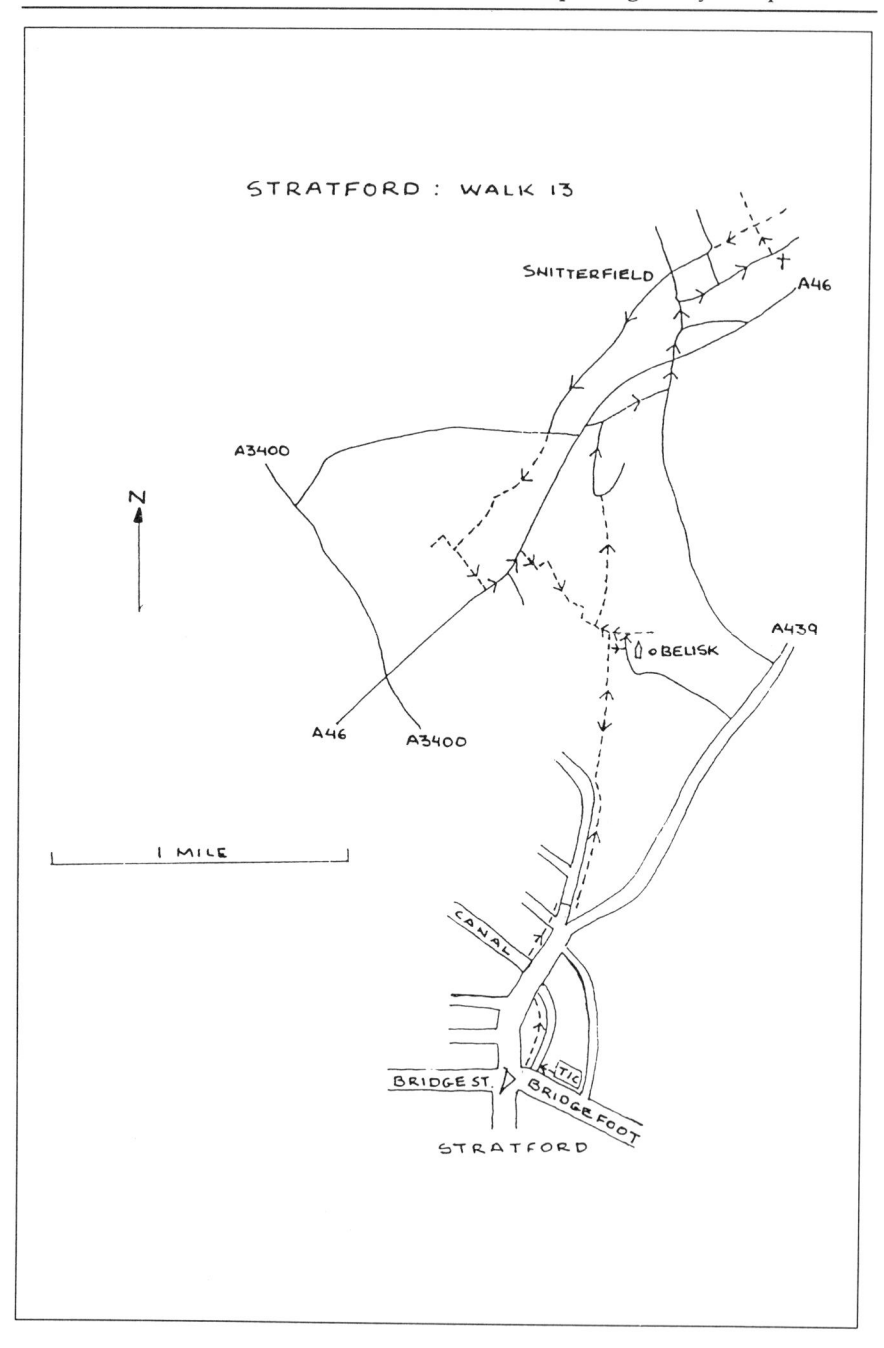

as you cross the road bridge over the canal. Near the start of the first pedestrian crossing, go right, down the steps to the canal path. Bear left, alongside the canal, as far as bridge 68, executing a bricked 'up and under', and then going immediately right, before lock 55, to the road.

Turn left, along the pavement – although rather early in the walk for nourishment, opposite you will see the Thai Kingdom Restaurant – 'Authentic Thai Cuisine' with offerings that include 'Khao Lad Naa Kang Puck' – a dish with hot Bardic connections. Further, take the road that forks left, initially Warwick Road, which soon changes to Welcombe Road, next crossing to the Church of St Gregory the Great where you should see a sign on the wall: 'Public path to Welcombe and Snitterfield'.

Continue as directed, north, along the right-hand pavement, eventually passing The Hill: 'Property of the Shakespeare Birthplace Trust' (no admission to the public).

Where Welcombe Road starts to curve left, go ahead, as indicated by the signed path: 'Ingon 2' – grassy underfoot, with a spot of mud in the winter months. The Welcombe Hill Obelisk may be seen in the distance. On through a metal kissing-gate, ideally bearing left slightly, away from the brambles, to another kissing-gate. You should come to a panel map of the Welcombe Hills (identical to the one seen during Walk 7) and another, as you start to ascend, passing on the right, the multi-chimneyed Welcombe Hotel. The Obelisk grows taller as you descend then ascend to a point level with the corner of a brick wall, then bear right, to a stile and up to:

The Welcombe Hill Obelisk

The Obelisk reaches to 120 feet and was erected in 1876 by Robert Needham Philips, in memory of his brother, Mark, who died in 1874. Mark Philips, a cotton manufacturer, started to build Welcombe House in 1866. It became the hotel that you have just passed in 1931. Read the tablets and enjoy the views. There are seats and tables for a breezy picnic.

Back at the stile, proceed north, bearing left at the junction and on through the gate (blue arrow-head on a post). A few metres further, a path joins via a third kissing-gate on the left. The walk returns that way (later, or now, if you have had enough exercise for one day). Continue to a second gate (blue and yellow arrow-heads this time), the start of the circular route that includes Snitterfield.

Bear right, before the gate, direction north, walking across the field, keeping the hedge to your left, to another gate and Ingon Manor Golf Course. Walkers are requested to stay on the public footpath to a round-topped stile; cross this and continue to a pair of stiles a metre or so apart – round-top and plank. An arrow-head on a post shows the way, over the footbridge, not following the path to your right, but continuing ahead into the next field.

Onward, still north, eventually taking the railway sleeper over the ditch (may be slippery), a stile and along, a line of trees to your right. You should reach a post with a green disc and white arrow on it that directs left: a few metres only, passing through the gap in the hedge to a curving track. Bear left, tracking north-west, soon veering north to a point east of north, with apple trees on either side. The fruit picking season is just about over; a few Cox's Orange Pippin remain. Tarmac underfoot, now, as you pass a packing plant with an arrow-head on its wall. A last left brings you to the entrance of Snitterfield Fruit Farm and the road.

Constantly 'car wary', turn right along what is Kings Lane (there is a grass verge in places), passing aptly named Uporchard (B & B), ignoring the path to your left, and walking as far as the T-junction, where the pavement begins. Bear left, signed Snitterfield and Warwick, still Kings Lane – on over the busy A46, eventually taking the road on your left, opposite the War Memorial, signed Snitterfield, Wolverton and Bearley. Again, watch for traffic, there is no pavement for a while, and then only a narrow one. White Horse Hill becomes Smiths Lane and, just past the 'mini-market', go right into Church Road, making for the Church of St James the Great, Snitterfield.

Briefly: first, before entering, you may wish to go around to the south side for a time check with the sundial on the wall. There is a bit of a tilt to it, but it is accurate to within half an hour. Through the west door beneath the tower, framed notes on the right give the necessary detail. You will also see a drawing of the church by Capt. J. Saunders dating from about 1810. Additionally, on this south wall, are baptismal and burial records of members of the Shakespeare family. On the north side, you may be lucky enough to purchase a leaflet (keenly priced, I took the penultimate); as well as describing the church, it reveals Shakespearean associations with the church and village, to which I might add part of Walk 5's Family Tree:

Going back a few generations, John Shakespeare, the Bard's father, was the son of Richard Shakespeare, who farmed as a tenant on land in the district, owned, incidentally, by Robert Arden of Wilmcote (see Walk 14). Some time before 1552, John Shakespeare moved to Stratford. Mary Arden, one of Robert Arden's daughters from his first marriage (the youngest of eight), married John Shakespeare about 1557, quite possibly in the Church of St John the Baptist, Aston Cantlow (see Walk 15). Significantly, in 1564, their third child and first son, William, was born.

Walking along the tiled floor of the nave, there is a fourteenth century arcade on either side; a clerestory rises above. Note the 'almost flat' oak roof 'erected when the clerestory was added in the fourteenth century', according to the leaflet.

Looking back and up, where the bell ropes are loosely curled – hatchments – one on each of the north and south walls. Approaching the chancel, on the south side, there is a fourteenth century font with heads carved in stone.

Entering the chancel with its 'oak trussed rafter roof', the choir stalls with end tracery, and a coat of arms at the east end of the south main stalls. The oak of the Jacobean communion rail is polished to a rich, dark brown (I remember a pleasantly lingering smell). There is also much eye-catching stained glass: the east window, for example, depicting Saxon saints, as described in both the leaflet and framed notes. I particularly liked the lighter colouring of the first window on the south side. Finally, in the south-east corner, you will see a double piscina.

Back at the road, go right for about twenty metres, taking the path opposite (close to a disc on a telegraph pole). Walking north-west through the wonky kissing-gate, then not going left but continuing ahead, to the right of the pond/lake, and over the footbridge. Next bear left, the hedge to your left, direction south-west across the field, through another gate and along the lane, quite muddy in the winter months. The tarmac begins near a timber-framed house as you proceed to the 'main' road. Plenty of signs: you have just walked along Brookside and are now at Wolverton Road. Bell Lane, with its 'Weak Ridge' warning is on the left. Cross, moving ahead along the curve of Wolverton Road, still south-west, towards the centre of the village.

There is a bus stop by the school at the crossroads (the start

Church of St James the Great, Snitterfield

of School Road), if you want to return directly to Stratford [see Public Transport]. The Foxhunter is to the left; the Snitterfield Arms is further to the right [see Refreshments].

Here, it is possible to walk by path and road west to Wilmcote. The route is not described; a better bus/canal option is given in Walk 14.

From the point of view of this walk: at the bus stop, cross to The Green and a long stretch of narrow road – spidery Cobwebs, Laburnum Cottage, Japonica Cottage and even Blossom Cottage – arachnids, trees, shrubs and flowers, leaving Snitterfield and eventually reaching the T-junction of Gospel Oak Lane.

Scale the stile opposite, walking roughly south, as directed by the arrow-head into a second field. A 'piped' footbridge leads to a third field, initially quite narrow. Move to the right-hand hedge (mind the ditch) and along, walking southwest, veering west, as far as a yellow arrow-head on a post that directs towards the left-hand hedge. Go on to where the hedge ends and yet another arrow-head on a post points south-west across a prairie. At the opposing hedge (passing to the left of the trees), you should see a post complete with arrow-heads. About twenty metres to its right sits a stile; ignore this and bear left, south-east, with the hedge to your right, still in this huge field. Reaching the corner, pass through the wooden gate to the busy A46. Cross with much care, going ahead for twenty metres or so, then left, along what remains of the road from Snitterfield to Lower Ingon. Once more approaching the A46, follow the right-hand pavement to just before a cyclepath. On the right, you should see, posted, a large green disc and the words: 'Public Bridleway'.

Astride the horse, bear right, south-east, along the lane. Further, the Obelisk appears, almost as an extra tall chimney of a distant farm. Beyond this farm there is a gate, coming at last to another gate and completion of the circle. Ignore the right-hand path, going through the gate. The circle starts to the left, north, but you advance towards the Obelisk, taking the kissing-gate on the right (the third-mentioned, earlier in the walk), retracing your steps to Stratford.

Walk 14: Wilmcote

Route: TIC – canal path – Wilmcote – canal path – TIC.

Distance: Up to 6 miles.

Maps: O.S. Landranger 151. O.S. Pathfinder 997.

Start: The TIC in Bridgefoot.

Terrain: Level, apart from an easy ascent alongside the Wilmcote Flight. The canal path can be muddy in places in winter. Only one stile! Bridge and lock walking by numbers, in reverse. The walk takes about an hour one-way.

Access: If you decide to drive separately to Wilmcote, entering Stratford along the last stretch of the A422, take the road on the left (opposite the Esso garage), signed Bishopston and Wilmcote. There is also a Mary Arden's House sign. The route is well posted from then on.

Parking: There is a free car park at Mary Arden's House, provided only for visitors to the property. If not visiting, one could park elsewhere in the village (often busy between spring and autumn).

Public Transport: Best of all is the Guide Friday bus which journeys regularly between Wilmcote and Stratford, and provides a commentary as well. The direct route is from Wilmcote to Stratford. There is a railway station in Wilmcote – refer to the General Information prologue.

Refreshments: Mary Arden's House. The Swan House Inn – food, Hook Norton bitter ('Hookie'), Theakston's XB and guest beers. The Masons Arms offers food, 'Hookie' and Newquay Steam, with an open coal fire in the winter – very welcome to cold weather walkers. There is a Post Office and mini-market for DIY snacks.

Walk 14: Wilmcote 97

Toilets: Pubs or in Mary Arden's House, but for the latter, you will have to shell out the pounds to get in and use them.

What you will see: Mary Arden's House and Countryside Museum, and lots of water.

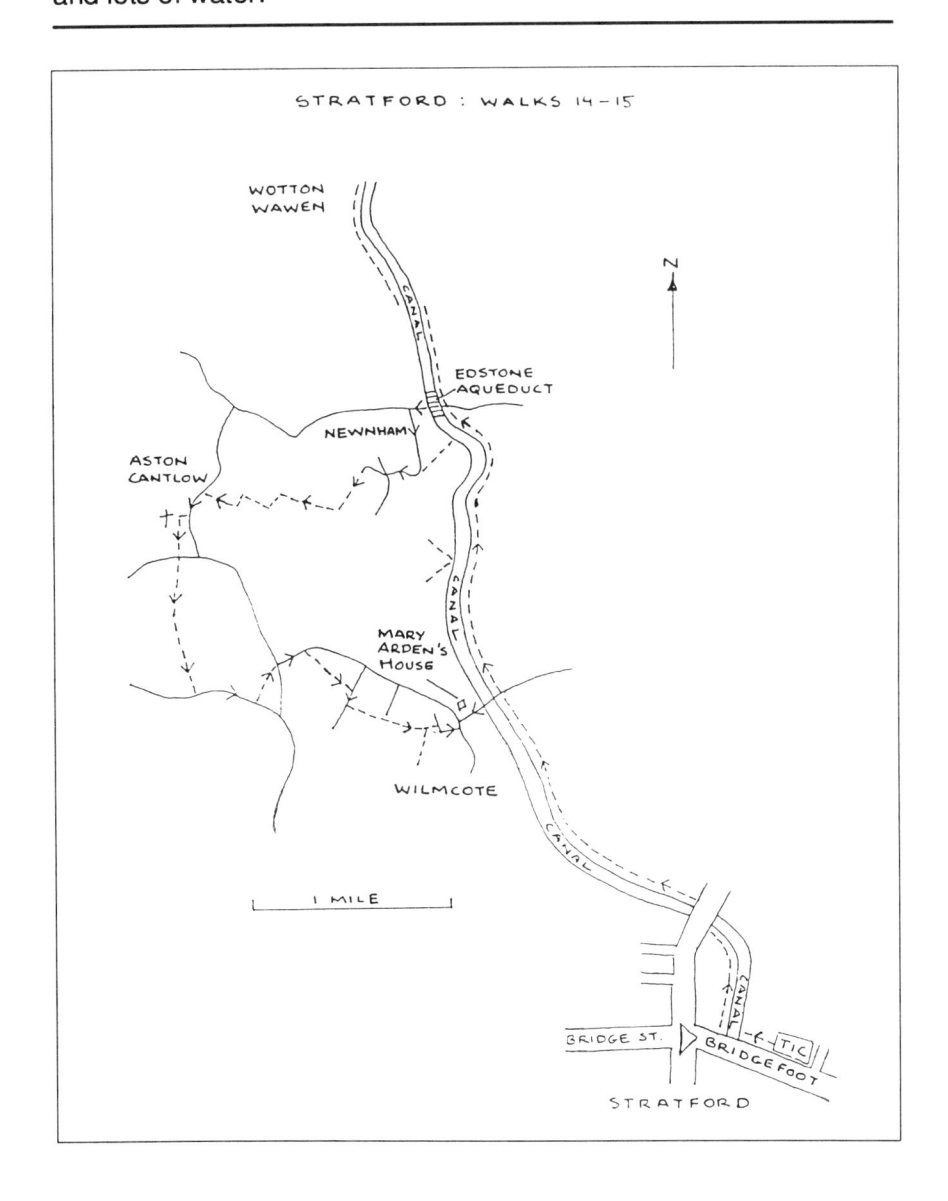

The Stratford-upon-Avon Canal

This is a ribbon of water, 25½ miles long, built at a cost of £297,000. It starts with Lock 1 at King's Norton, which connects with the Worcester and Birmingham Canal, flows through Kingswood Junction, where a separate Lock 20 allows access to the Grand Union Canal, and ends at Lock 56 – the far end of Stratford's Canal Basin, entering the River Avon.

The story of the canal opens in 1793 with an Act of Parliament approving its construction. Cutting (picks and shovels) began at Kings Norton in November of the same year. A notice on the wall of the canal cottage near Lock 40 (passed during the walk) will tell you that work was delayed several times due to lack of funds (a warring French Emperor who met his Waterloo on 18th June, 1815, was ultimately responsible), the canal being completed through to the Avon on 24th June, 1816.

Trade, including the carriage of coal, limestone and agricultural produce, increased with the passing of the years. Unfortunately, the combined efforts of other competing canals, the introduction of rail and road improvements led to an inexorable decline – fewer and fewer boats – which in turn resulted in a deterioration of the fabric of the canal, to a point where it became virtually unnavigable. Virtually, but not quite; for this is when, in 1958, Bridge 59 (at Wilmcote) played an important part in its continued existence. In that year, Warwickshire County Council applied for a 'Warrant of Abandonment', wanting to knock down the bridge and run the road across the canal bed. Thanks to the Stratford-upon-Avon Canal Society, however, part-navigation was proven by canoe and the canal saved. Eventually, and mainly through the efforts of volunteers, the canal was restored, to be reopened by 'Queen Elizabeth The Queen Mother 11th July, 1964' (see the notice at Avon/Canal Lock 56, walked in Walk 2).

For the full story, invest in: 'The Stratford-upon-Avon Canal Guide', available from the TIC.

The Walk

The walk to bridge 68 is as for Snitterfield's Walk 13; thumb the pages and, at the TIC, go west, young and not-so-young walker, past the Pen and Parchment and entrance to Bancroft Place, crossing the road bridge to a point close to the start of the first pedestrian crossing, taking the steps down to the canal path. Bear left, as far as bridge 68, executing a bricked 'up and under', then leaving the Snitterfield route, continuing along the canal path.

There is a succession of bridges and locks: past locks 55 and 54, under bridge 67 that leads up to Great William Street, by lock 53 to a street map. Bridge 66 carries Clopton Road; bridge 65, the wide and busy Birmingham Road. Leaving the centre of the town, there are signs of industry; pass lock 52 and go under two railway bridges and bridge 64 (Timothy's Bridge Road) then a longish stretch to lock 51. The industrial estates give way to new housing and, much easier on the eye, (slightly) rolling fields.

Approaching bridge 63, the railway line parallels on the right – perhaps surfacing for air beyond this bridge for a look at Victoria Spa Lodge. Back on the canal path, the opportunity to take on drinking water, but only if navigating a narrow boat, which is unlikely. No problem with the date of bridge 62A, 'Chaly Beate'; soon beginning the moderate ascent alongside the Wilmcote Flight.

A series of 11 locks, numbers 50-40, in three groups of three, five and three, requiring strong arms and much patience if taking the wet route. Next to lock 44 stands a canal cottage;

after about fifty metres you will pass a small, grassy, metal bridge (number 61). Finally, just beyond lock 40, a second canal cottage with a notice on its wall telling you about The Stratford Canal Story, The People, The Cottage and Canals Today. Why not take a breather and read all about it?

Leaving the Wilmcote Flight, proceed under bridge 60, the start of another long stretch – housing on the far side – to and under bridge 59 (originally the one that was nearly demolished in 1958), where an information panel also tells you about the canal; more for boaters than walkers. Here, go immediately right, over the only stile of the walk, to Station Road.

The railway station is further to the left; bearing right will take you into Wilmcote and:

Mary Arden's House and Countryside Museum

The timber-framed house, which dates from the early part of the sixteenth century, is assumed to have been the home of Mary Arden, the Bard's mother, before her marriage to John Shakespeare. Quite possibly, they were married in Aston Cantlow's Church of St John the Baptist in the year 1557, or thereabouts. St John's is visited during Walk 15.

Large families were the norm in those days. Robert Arden had eight daughters from his first marriage; Mary was the youngest. He married a second time, there being no children from this marriage. John and Mary also had eight children: William was their third child and first-born son.

The Arden family was one of the few English families who could trace their line back to before William the Conqueror. The name was taken from an ancient forest, the Forest of Arden, which was used as background in William Shakespeare's 'As You Like It'.

The leaflet is a good buy, describing the fabric and furnish-

Mary Arden's House (detail)

ings of the house, and the museum, including nearby Glebe Farm. There are falconry displays, and a ducks, poultry and field walk: a full complement of farm animals can be seen. Additionally, one may browse a gift shop and dine a picnic area (away from the swooping hawks). As always, the staff are there to guide and assist.

Having viewed and still feeling thirsty or peckish, bear right with a roadside view of the house and signs of restoration, as far as the T-junction. Opposite is The Swan House Inn; adjoining Dosthill Cottage offers B & B. Going right, past the Post Office and mini-market, will bring you to The Masons Arms [see Refreshments].

Brimful of drink, food and history, one may now return along the canal path to Stratford (absolutely not a tedious repeat). Alternatively, take the Guide Friday bus or train [see Public Transport]. For still more exercise, try Walk 15 to Aston Cantlow; it starts here, at Wilmcote.

Lastly, a note for exceptionally determined walkers. A possible route from Wilmcote that treks south to Shottery via Billesley and Drayton exists. It is (at the time of writing) part-unsigned, and in places is marred by much traffic and mud. I have neither described nor marked it on the map.

Walk 15: Aston Cantlow

Route: Wilmcote – Edstone Aqueduct – Newnham – Aston Cantlow – Wilmcote.

Distance: Up to 6 miles.

Maps: O.S. Landranger 151. O.S. Pathfinder 997.

Start: The Guide Friday stop adjacent to Mary Arden's House.

Terrain: Level, apart from descents at the Edstone Aqueduct and the lane beyond Newnham. Also one short, stepped ascent – a diverted section, near the end of the walk. In the winter months, mud in places along the canal path; one may wallow in the stuff beyond Newnham, and this may be avoided by walking a reduced linear route between Wilmcote and the aqueduct.

Access and Parking: See Walk 14 if you decide to drive separately to Wilmcote.

Public Transport: Bus 228 between Stratford and Aston Cantlow, Mondays to Saturdays. The Guide Friday bus runs between Stratford and Wilmcote. There is a railway station in Wilmcote. See the Travel Guide and General Information prologue.

Refreshments: In Aston Cantlow, Home Farm Stores provides tea, coffee and sandwiches; the King's Head offers food and a selection of beers – Boddington's and Wadworth's 6X, for example, and a cat on the mat (sitting in front of a log fire in the winter).

Toilets: Pubs at Aston Cantlow. See Walk 14 regarding Wilmcote.

What you will see: The Edstone Aqueduct; A brief description of the Church of St John the Baptist at Aston Cantlow is given; another church with Shakespearean associations.

The Walk

NOTE: please refer to the map for Walk 14.

From the Guide Friday stop adjacent to Mary Arden's House, proceed to Station Road and bear left, crossing the canal bridge and then going immediately left, over the stile down to the canal. Turn right, north, along the canal path.

A morning in January – there has been a severe frost during the night, almost the first of an unusually (so far) mild winter. Swans on ice, seen at the Canal Basin in Stratford, earlier; even the canal is icebound. The sun shines, but without warmth, low in a pale blue sky. Frosted trees and good walking weather; the expected mud has become hard underfoot, albeit a mite slippery in places.

So much for the elements as you perambulate to bridge 58. On the far side are two arrow-heads: the left-hand path would take you back to Wilmcote; the other to Newnham. Still on the canal path, soon passing a winding hole, where the narrow boats do an about-turn. The canal curves to the right. The clickety-clack of a train to the east, sounding twice as loud in the cold air. Canal recurve, eventually passing crumbling, brick bridge 57. The path on the other side would also take you to Newnham. Onward to:

The Edstone Aqueduct

This is substantial and impressive: an early nineteenth century iron trough of water – one of the largest/longest in the country – that extends to over 475 feet. As you will see, it leaks slightly on this side.

If you want to avoid the possibility of mud to come, an easier option, now, is to retrace your steps to Wilmcote. Alternatively, walk across the aqueduct, continuing along the canal

The Edstone Aqueduct

path to Wootton Wawen, bearing in mind that you will have to return (the X20 bus would take you from WW back to Stratford).

At this point, take the steps down to your right, before the aqueduct, to the road, then going left along the grass verge, under the iron, between its supporting brick pillars. Further, bear left – the road is signed to Newnham – veering west (the path noted at bridge 57 joins here), approaching housing and entering the village.

Keep to the main route, ignoring turnings to left and right. Beyond the last house, 'Lamb's Cot', the tarmac disappears to be replaced by signs of horses, even tyre marks, curving left and muddily along, walking in a south-westerly direction. Continue ahead at the field, with the hedge to your left, next following the line of the path/track around to the right, west, on through a gap in the opposing hedge, and ahead, the hedge to your right. In the far right-hand corner of this second field, you come to the start of what can be an extremely muddy section. Go down and around, perhaps avoiding the worst bits by moving to the left, descending to a field. Making progress, the hedge to your right, cornering, soon going right, through a gap in the hedge. The grassy strip of a last field (for a while) brings you to Bearley Road and Aston Cantlow. A public footpath white arrow on a green disc should point the way you have just come.

Turn left, eventually passing (opposite) Home Farm Stores [see Refreshments], and on this side, Aston Cantlow Club with its sunny sign. There is a bus stop at the entrance to Guild Road [see Public Transport]. Then comes timber-framed Guild House, which dates from the early sixteenth century, and adjoining Guild Cottage and Guild Corner. Though the last two are brick, they were built at about the same time; timbers go through all three. Guild House is now used as a village hall with new, twentieth century parts tacked on at the back.

Cross to the King's Head [see Refreshments] and at the corner, bear right along Church Lane to the churchyard. Just beyond the entrance are two arrow-heads on a post. Follow the right-hand one to the south porch of the Church of St John the Baptist. But remember the other arrow-head, you will return here after browsing the church to continue the walk.

The church is open during the 'lighter months', so I was told. A notice board at the entrance to the churchyard gives details of where a key may be obtained.

The 'Shakespeare Connection' in the soon-to-be-purchased church guide tells you about the marriage of John Shakespeare and Mary Arden. It is a possibility that they were married here about 1557; unfortunately, the church registers began after that year.

Briefly (as the guide reveals), St John's has origins in Norman, possibly Saxon times, and was restored in the mid-nineteenth century. Approaching the porch and looking up at the battlemented tower, with thirteenth and fourteenth century stages, and a pinnacle at each corner. Entering, above and to the left are the organ and gallery. Crossing the nave, go under an arch of the arcade to the north side and the fifteenth century font. Counting and noting the sides of the octagonal bowl: three out of four carved heads of men remain, one or two with chins of bristly stone. Close by, an opportunity to purchase the guide and notelets. In this north-west corner, an 'ogee-arched' door leads to a turret (you can get a better view from the outside).

Walking east along the north aisle to the Guild Chapel; its window, depicting Christ in Majesty, contains fragments of ancient glass. Here, one may move beneath the arcade to the thirteenth century chancel. Set in the south wall are three sedilia and a piscina. Leaving the chancel (arch rebuilt during the restoration), pass the wooden pulpit, emerging via the south porch, going around to the right for a look at the truncated turret, and away.

Return to the post, following the direction indicated by the left-hand arrow-head, over the stile and along, a footbridge straddling the ditch, a stile in the fence, striking roughly south across the field. Sheep stand and stare – with their home-grown, warm, woolly coats, they can well afford to. One more stile brings you to the road.

The AC village sign is nearby. Proceed along the unsurfaced lane opposite, still south. Further, where the lane bears right, continue ahead, the hedge to your right, to yet another stile and road. Turn left, walking east – seeking an arrow-head on a post on this left-hand side. And there it is, in company of a stile, allowing you to go north-east across the field to the junction. Here, take the road opposite, signed to Wilmcote and Mary Arden's House, passing Aston Holdings, currently offering farm fresh eggs and oven ready turkeys for sale.

Beyond white railings (on either side of the road – a stream runs under), you should see a Caravan Club sign on a gate to your right. There is no arrow-head, but a stile in the far hedge confirms the route. The gate has an odd combination of bolt, chain and hook, yet opens quite easily. Walking south-east across the field, nimbly over the stile into a second field to an arrow-head on a post, which directs right to another pointing left, through a gap in the hedge. Follow the winding path to the only ascent of the walk – mounting steps – scaling the stiles (arrow-heads and path diverted discs), eventually arriving at a 'semi-surfaced' lane.

An arrow-head points right for a few metres, as far as the bungalow, Uplands (big 28), where you take the signed path on your left. A kissing-gate opens to a muddy patch of ground, by stables and one inquisitive horse to another kissing-gate, and along the field, the hedge to your left, a point south of east. On through a gap to a second field. Ditto third and fourth fields, passing a post (green disc and white arrow), and after about twenty metres, selecting the left fork, the hedge, as ever, to your left, walking east, finally reaching the back gardens of a row of bungalows. There are (hopefully) three arrow-heads on the wooden fencing – just continue ahead, between the fencing to the road. Wending right and left will take you to the Swan House Inn at the corner. Proceed along the road opposite, back to Mary Arden's House and walk end.

Walk 16: Charlecote

Route: TIC – Clopton Bridge – Loxley Road – Alveston Farm – Hunscote – Charlecote.

Distance: About 5 miles, one-way.

Maps: O.S. Landranger 151. O.S. Pathfinder 998.

Start: The TIC in Bridgefoot.

Terrain: Level with a full quota of mud.

Access: Should you decide to drive and visit separately – cross the Clopton Bridge, going roughly east, away from Bridgefoot, next taking the first left, the B4086, as indicated by the Charlecote Park sign. The route is well-signed from then on.

Parking: There is a car park nearly opposite the entrance to Charlecote Park.

Public Transport: Bus 18 runs between Stratford and Charlecote: hourly Monday to Saturday, every two hours on a Sunday. The stop in Charlecote is a few metres along the road signed Wellesbourne.

Refreshments: The Charlecote Pheasant Country Hotel offers a selection of food, draught Bass and antique fairs throughout the year (six in 1995). There is an 'Orangery Restaurant' in Charlecote Park.

Toilets: Pubs and in Charlecote Park.

What you will see: Charlecote Park; A brief description of the Church of St Leonard is given; Light aircraft, helicopters and (possibly) a Vulcan bomber.

110 Exploring Stratford-upon-Avon

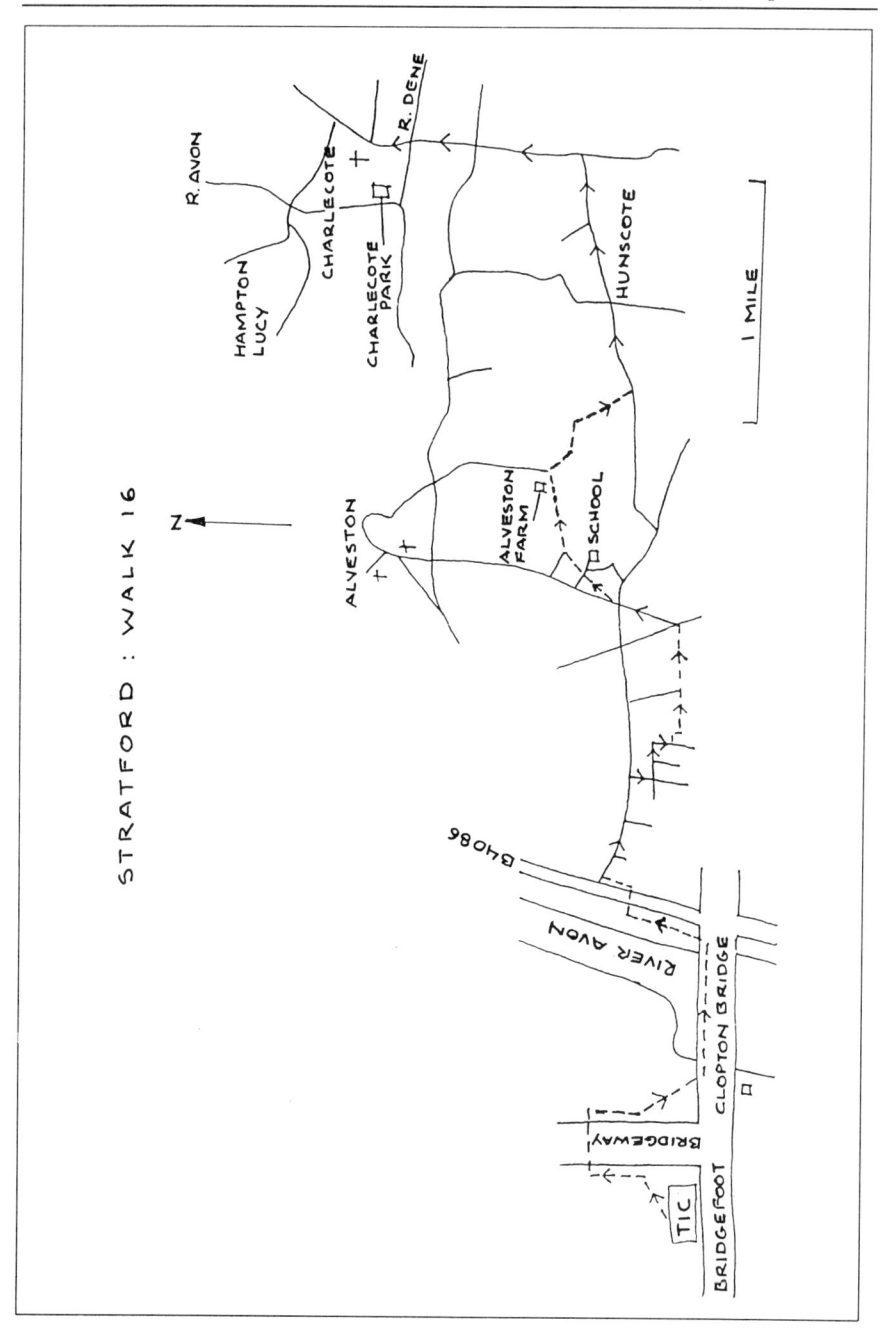

The Walk

The first part of the walk to the start of Clopton Bridge is as for Walk 7. So, cross the bridge, the narrow pedestrian walkway, taking the road on your left, the B4086, signed Tiddington, Wellesbourne and Charlecote Park. Walking the left-hand pavement and looking towards the Avon, you can see Walk 7's arched concrete footbridge. Later, cross with care to Bridgetown Stores and Post Office, soon bearing right, along the road signed Loxley; in fact, Loxley Road. This is a long stretch of gardened suburbia that passes Saxon Close, Stratford's rugby ground and Manor Road – lined with conifers, bare branches, and a sprinkling of flowers encouraged by a mild February – pink almonds, Skimmias, yellow Cytisus and daffodils, and red-berried Cotoneasters. The horticultural part of the walk.

Turn right into Avon Crescent, left along Burford Road and right at the mini-roundabout into Wootton Close. Advancing, take the public footpath to the left, signed Alveston Hill, on between the bungalows, east, to a field. Go right, south, with the hedge to your right, shortly bearing left, following the line of the path, resuming an easterly direction and staying just to the right of the hawthorn hedge. Approaching buildings, do not enter the yard, executing a swift right and left, again beside the hedge of the same large field. Much further, near the corner, climb the fence/stile to a path between housing, a stile and the road.

At this point, go right for a few metres, taking the road on your left, walking north-east, perhaps glancing to the north-west to see Walk 13's Welcombe Hill Obelisk piercing the horizon. Continue ahead at the crossroads, where about twenty metres of grass verge bring you to a public footpath on your right, signed to Alveston.

Scale the stile, forging ahead through the wooden gate and bearing left, along the edge of the playing field. Approaching an unsurfaced lane, make for a yellow arrow-head on a tree, north-east, and then another arrow-head on a post, across grass, with the brambly, wire/wooden fence to your right. Beyond the narrow, high-stepping stile in the corner, yet another arrow-head on a tree directs north-east, across the entrance to a house (dogs wag their tails and bark) to a white gate on the right (not entirely easy to open or close). The resultant path emerges onto a field.

Proceed a point north of east, along the left-hand edge of the field. Hedge-laying has just finished; a really neat job, too. Climb the stile, striking still a point north of east, as far as the south side of Alveston Farm, next moving south-east, making for a section of wooden fencing, beyond and to the left of a telegraph pole in this second field. Up and over, going across a third field, with the hedge to your left, direction east, and at the left-hand corner, bearing right, approximately south-east, the hedge eternally to your left. A last stile leads you to what can be exceptionally muddy Hunscote Lane. For reference, you should see a barn of sorts opposite and to the left slightly.

Squelch left, east, passing a semi-detached house, where the track 'firms up'. Further, for apiarists: four hives among the trees, striding ahead at the crossing – private signs on either side – another semi and the sound of barking from Hunscote Kennels to a T-junction.

Go left, north, towards Charlecote. You may have noticed the wind-sock a few minutes ago, and can now treat yourself to a road-side view of the light aircraft and helicopters on the airfield. The temptation of flying lessons on offer and, next to South Warwickshire School of Flying, there is the impressive sight of, at the time of writing, a Vulcan bomber. After obtaining permission, I wandered around and under this (to me) huge plane. 'Join us and learn to fly,' says a notice; probably not the Vulcan, though.

Vulcan bomber near Charlecote

Continue ahead with care at the crossroads, signed Charlecote and Warwick; conveniently, there is plenty of grass verge. The road gets busy in the summer, so exercise caution where it narrows at the bridge over the River Dene. Only a short step, now, to the entrance of:

Charlecote Park

Charlecote Park is administered by the National Trust. Briefly: the Lucys have occupied the estate since the thirteenth, possibly the twelfth century. The house you see today dates from the middle of the sixteenth century and underwent major restoration in the nineteenth century; its elaborate furnishings reflect the Elizabethan style. Within, a sample of the treat in store includes a Victorian kitchen and brewhouse, carriages and portraits of the Lucy family through the centuries. Without, a park by Capability Brown, the eighteenth century landscape gardener, with roaming red and fallow deer, and nibbling Jacob sheep. The park is open from April to the end of October. A guide book may be purchased at the gatehouse as you enter, and there is a National Trust shop.

On a Shakespeare theme, and according to local tradition, the young Bard helped himself to the occasional deer and rabbit, incurring the magisterial wrath of Sir Thomas Lucy.

Having explored, and back at the road, you may wish to follow the path, left, for a look at the church which is usually kept locked, though it may be open after services on Sundays. A notice at the entrance to the churchyard advises that keys may be obtained from Mr Fairfax-Lucy at The Malt House, opposite the Hampton Lucy turning (about 200 metres further north-east along the road). The 'key borrow' to this house takes about three minutes. Ring the bell below: 'The Malt House', on the wall facing the road. You will be asked for identification

Charlecote Park

– theft and vandalism are everywhere. Standing here and looking north-west, you should see the Church of St Peter at Hampton Lucy; not included in this walk, however.

The entrance to St Leonard's is via the door at the west end. Very briefly: the present church dates from the mid-nineteenth century, owing its existence (according to the leaflet to be 'purchased' shortly) to the efforts – financial and otherwise – of Mrs Mary Elizabeth Lucy who laid the foundation stone on 5th April, 1850. Inside stand an intricately carved font in the north-west corner, and the tub-shaped Norman font opposite. The leaflet is a good read, donations in the slot in the north wall, please. It really is worth the visit to view the tierceron vaulting as you walk east along the nave. Beyond the choir, in the north 'chapel', are tomb chests and effigies to members of the Lucy family; a description of each is given. Also, there are three hatchments high on the west wall.

And that is the end of the last walk. Don't forget to return the key through the letter-box near the bell. I prefer to walk to Charlecote, indulge in a pint of draught Bass, and get the bus back, though you could always retrace to Stratford. If you need a mite more exercise, a leaflet describes a walk within the park grounds (the numbered posts make a change from yellow arrow-heads).